## Praise for **Braggi**

"*Bragging Rights* will help you navigate one of the hardest things to do—talk about your success! This book is full of ideas to help you be seen and heard more, without the 'ick' factor."
**JOANNA ROTENBERG**, president of personal investing, Fidelity Investments

"Smart, kind, and useful, it's the sort of insight you'll be glad you paid attention to."
**SETH GODIN**, author, *This Is Marketing*

"If you want to know how to get unstuck and proudly share your work with the world, *Bragging Rights* is a must-read book with actionable advice on how to lead with confidence and tell your story."
**AMBER MAC**, award-winning podcaster, *#TheFeed* on SiriusXM

"The world is waiting for you. This book will help you take that step forward to be seen and heard so you can make the difference you want to see."
**KAREN GILL**, MBE, cofounder of everywoman

"You should be your greatest advocate. For practical, courageous ways to be seen and heard, this might be the book you're looking for."
**MICHAEL BUNGAY STANIER**, bestselling author, *The Coaching Habit* and *How to Begin*

"Lisa Bragg shines a perceptive light on the crucial role of advocating for yourself, especially if you are a woman. We won't succeed unless we articulate our value and contributions confidently and consistently. The practical advice in this well-researched book makes it clear that 'brag' is a *good* four-letter word! I will be implementing several of her suggestions."

**GENA COX**, author, *Leading Inclusion*

"What I really like is that this book is not just about how to talk about yourself (which Lisa Bragg does help you do). It's about how we can help each other shine."

**SANDI TRELIVING**, philanthropist and mental health advocate

"A must-read for everyone who has felt overlooked or undervalued, and for the leaders who want to help them shine. *Bragging Rights* will shift your mindset and uncover opportunities beyond your aspirations."

**SYBIL VERCH**, executive vice president, Raymond James Ltd.

"*Bragging Rights* gives you both permission and motivation to joyfully and authentically share your gifts. This book will help you open doors in your career, grow your business, and allow your work to make the biggest impact in the world."

**PAMELA SLIM**, award-winning author, *The Widest Net* and *Body of Work*

"Respect—this is a bold, honest, and very valuable book, not just for the individual readers, but also for our society. Having grown up with the Danish Jante law, I find this very refreshing. I love 'brag' being defined as 'spirited, brave, and proud.' Thank you for your leadership!"

**HELLE BANK JORGENSEN**, CEO and founder, Competent Boards

"After being raised to believe that working hard and showing up well would always be recognized, self-promoting felt wrong to me. I was in my early forties when I realized I needed to talk more about my own success. After working with Lisa Bragg in one of her workshops, I found a way to do so that felt authentic. *Bragging Rights* thoughtfully offers Lisa's same insights in an easy-to-digest formula that any professional or entrepreneur should consider."
**LAURA REINHOLZ**, head of customer experience, IMO, BMO Financial Group

"I don't know anyone who doesn't struggle with acknowledging their success, especially women. *Bragging Rights* is well researched and filled with exercises and tips to help form your dialogue about your success. I particularly loved the chapter on how to self-promote; it will be a section I turn to whenever I go to an event where I have to speak about myself."
**ISAAC BOOTS**, fitness philanthropist, founder of TORCH'D

"Warning: Engaging with this book may cause you to walk taller and shine brighter. How are you different? What is your superpower? Can you answer these questions about yourself? *Bragging Rights* thoughtfully provides tools and context to help you really see and celebrate YOU."
**JULIE HANSEN**, vice president and global executive advisor, Salesforce

**BRAGGING RIGHTS**

# BRAGGING

# RIGHTS

How to Talk about Your Work
Using Purposeful Self-Promotion

**LISA BRAGG**

Copyright © 2023 by Lisa Bragg

All rights reserved. No part of this book may be reproduced, stored in a retrieval system or transmitted, in any form or by any means, without the prior written consent of the publisher, except in the case of brief quotations, embodied in reviews and articles.

Some names and identifying details have been changed to protect the privacy of individuals.

Cataloguing in publication information is available from Library and Archives Canada.
ISBN 978-1-77458-279-4 (paperback)
ISBN 978-1-77458-280-0 (ebook)
ISBN 978-1-77458-346-3 (audiobook)

Page Two
pagetwo.com

Edited by Kendra Ward
Copyedited by Steph VanderMeulen
Cover and interior design by Taysia Louie

lisabragg.com

*Thank you to all the people who cheered me on while I wrote this book. I appreciate you.*

*Jason, thank you for always helping me shine brighter.*

*Elora, thank you for being my biggest cheerleader.*

# Contents

Introduction: A Call to Hidden Gems  1

PART ONE **RECLAIMING BRAGGING RIGHTS**  11

1. A Case for Bragging  15
2. A Legacy of Hiding  31
3. How Power Plays In  45
4. How We Are at Odds  57
5. Programming Is Reality and Myth  73
6. The Need to Partner  87

PART TWO **HOW TO OWN YOUR BRAGGING RIGHTS**  99

7. How to Self-Promote  105
8. Brag with Purpose  131
9. Know What Makes You Remarkable  143
10. Own Your Knowledgeable Authority  153
11. Know Who You Are  169
12. Help People Talk about You  179
13. Lead Others to Shine  189
14. No Longer a Hidden Gem  207

Conclusion: Call to Greatness  219

Bonus Material  223

Acknowledgments  227

Notes  229

# Introduction
# A Call to Hidden Gems

BACK IN 2007, young Justin Bieber was putting his first videos on YouTube, and I was a TV reporter who met the future megastar and a few of his friends on a street in his hometown of Stratford, Ontario, Canada.

The barely teenage boys were begging me to let them be on camera, but the story was about politics. Bieber told me about his YouTube fame and then sang to me—I was seriously impressed. He was already in early talks with producers I had never heard of. This kid was going places fast. Back at the TV station, I told the CHCH news assignment manager that we needed to do a story on this boy who was racking up followers on YouTube with his voice. Opportunity was knocking for him. Usually, when I pitched a story, I'd get to do it, but this one landed with a thud. It was a resounding no, along with scorn that I'd even suggested a YouTube story.

I realized Bieber was on to something, though. He had picked himself and put himself out there, and people were responding. He didn't need the assignment manager's approval. I realized that soon people wouldn't necessarily need gatekeepers like the assignment manager to allow them to get into other people's hearts and minds. Soon after this incident, I quit news to start a content company.

In the early days of MediaFace, my content company, I helped leaders, experts, and visionaries within organizations get their ideas to their audiences through video, and the videos we created were among the first the organizations hosted on their websites. After meetings, on the always-productive walk to the elevator where much more business is done, the leader of the initiative inevitably would ask me, "How can I get myself out there too?" They knew they were being passed over for opportunities because they weren't the loudest in the room or they felt they politically needed to be subtle but ended up invisible. When I'm hired as a thinking partner for executives nowadays, we often look at the stories people tell themselves and others. Far too often, I point out that people want to do business, and work, for other humans. When we're involved with you, we want to know that you are the real deal. Just talking about the company doesn't work, and when you avoid, diminish, or hide your personal successes, it costs you or the company fortunes and untold opportunities.

Bragging and self-promotion are no longer reserved for only a few. There's been a shift in our world of work: we all now need to do it. If it's not second nature to you (it isn't for me), then you might feel on the spot, awkward, and even perhaps icky when you need to do it. Why is that?

I was told the secret to success when I was young, and I believed it wholeheartedly: "Be a good girl, put your head down, do good work, and eventually someone will notice you." This four-step secret worked amazingly well while I was in school. In the world of work, though, this secret to success is more like a secret to being looked over. It keeps you stuck.

Or perhaps you know another school formula: "If I just get this one more certificate, credential, client, or project, my reputation will soar" (cue the trumpets!). Even before the certificate arrives, we feel as if we need to reach another level, holding on to the belief that one day someone will notice we're the expert. But here's a hint: you already are an expert. During my interviews for this book, I found that some people who look and sound like leaders to the rest of us actually find that mantle too big. Know that at some point we all follow and we all lead.

If you're nodding at any of this, know you're not alone; I'm right along with you, and so are the majority of the people who attend my workshops and keynotes. These statements and myths, however, hamper you: they keep you from the opportunities you already deserve.

## The World Needs You

There's something I know about you that you may not know about yourself. You are the source of so many great things. The world needs you. We need your spark for the full-on fireworks you can bring, or that little combustion you can deliver to that one person in your community or across the globe to help them soar. You have more to offer than you know. You have more to give than has ever been given.

You've kept quiet when you have something (significant) to share because you don't want to come off as obnoxious, or you are afraid of the penalties, or you simply don't know how to communicate in a way that makes you feel comfortable. You grew up with influences from an era that didn't openly accept bragging or self-promotion. While you are far from average, you were told you weren't special. But as Maya Angelou so beautifully puts it, true arrogance is "in denying one's own specialness—and denying the specialness of others."

## Be Successful, But Don't Talk about Success

According to my data, we know we need to talk about our successes to get ahead, but we're caught in a paradox. We're told to brag without bragging, which means "be successful without talking about your success." It simply doesn't make sense. You can't sell a secret.

The good news is that when people hear or see someone bragging, my research shows that 85 percent are ready to "cheer you on"; only 13 percent of the respondents said they'd "ignore you," and 2 percent said they'd "turn around and brag about themselves." So, the vast majority of us are really cheering for you.

To be seen and heard is a fundamental part of the human experience, but society puts odd limits on this, for some people. For the past few hundred years, cultures have demanded that some people act like hidden gems, while others, those in dominant organizational or social groups, are put in the spotlight, often through minimal effort on their part.

Self-promotion or bragging shouldn't be reserved for the people who hold control and reinforce it using statements like, "Your work should speak for itself." Whether to avoid being invisible, to stay employed, to get a new position, or to solve impossible challenges, everyone needs to build social currency, which is a form of capital whose value is measured by your ability to influence conversations and outcomes—for yourself and others. But women especially have been trained to be quiet, play small, and wait to be chosen. Some people are free to talk wildly about their success, while others are told that to do so is distasteful, punishable, almost an offense.

In a time of global companies, international networks, social media, and immigration, society needs to recognize more than ever that self-promotion is good so that those with ideas to share can step forward. It's time to reconsider how we gain, give, and use status. It's time to normalize talking about success and our work using purposeful self-promotion.

## A Call to Hidden Gems

The goal of this book isn't to fix you. You're already awesome. You are meant to shine, but you might be feeling disappointed, as if you're invisible and your contributions don't have the level of impact you thought they would. I wrote this book as a guide to help you discover and consider the spiderweb of external and internal forces that hold you back, so you can then move forward by talking about your accomplishments, success, status, and by (cheer)leading others. This work is not about how you outperform your rivals. Think "collaboration" instead of "competition."

The stories throughout this book are of people like you and me. They are my clients, my friends. I also share stories about my own life. If you can see it, you can be it—or at least be empowered to make your own path.

Many books on self-promotion point to big brands for examples on how to do it, but you're not a big brand. Big-brand marketing lessons aren't going to help you. You're a human having a human experience. You need social currency to work for you. You've already done the hard work. Time to tell people about it in a way that will help you shine.

And don't worry. In reading this book and doing this work, you won't become a puffed-up version of yourself who will turn everyone off. Quite the opposite. I'm going to give you constraints so that you avoid going to the extreme of self-promotion: being opportunistic, self-centered, oblivious. You already know that you're not the center of the universe. You already know that you're not the sole author of your accomplishments. This isn't a conceited, fake, ego-gratifying process of spending hours a day working on your "brand." It is, however, about no longer being the best-kept secret and about letting the people who need you know you're here to serve.

My goal is that you learn to model what success, achievement, and performance look like in the infinite ways they appear so that your peers, too, can see it and be it, and the next generation has a more effortless experience. My mission is to help you be seen and heard so that you get the opportunities you deserve.

## Grounded in Research

In the development of this book, I undertook what's now one of the world's most extensive international studies on bragging and self-promotion. Before 2012, very little was written or researched on bragging. Past articles point to research studies that warn how bad it is for people, especially women, to brag. It was "bad" and there were "dire consequences." But that research on bragging and self-promotion doesn't necessarily reflect experienced professionals. Most of the studies were based on small samples that comprised university students. When we're younger, we have an especially high desire to fit in, so we often want to avoid anything that will make us stand out, such as bragging. Other participants were paid extremely

It's time to reconsider
how we gain, give,
and use status.

low fees for filling out a survey. These are very different groups from the audience of professionals who read the leadership and business publications where the studies are reported. Often, the studies also fail to express a definition of bragging or leave it open to interpretation by the participants. And it is a highly nuanced word.

I undertook this research to reflect a more experienced and professional audience and included an online survey (through social media platforms and networks, over email, and on research portals) and a follow-up contact option with selected participants. The survey questions looked at self-promotion, bragging, self-advocacy, humility, modesty, culture, and society. There were multiple-choice questions, and respondents could elect to expand responses with longer answers. It took between ten and thirty minutes to complete. The survey information was collected anonymously, with more than half of the respondents self-selecting to share their contact information for a follow-up interview.

At the time of this writing, more than four hundred people from twenty-three countries have participated. Responses came from people who self-identified as women, men, female, male, lesbian, nonbinary, human, and queer. While not specifically asked, many people identified a range of religious affiliations. Many people chose to identify their economic status; respondents came from a full range of backgrounds, from extreme poverty to affluence. People identified as neurodivergent, disabled, or able-bodied. However, the data available on various intersecting identities is too limited to delineate. People were between eighteen and seventy-four years old, with only a small number of eighteen- to twenty-four-year-olds responding. The people who responded were middle and upper managers, CEOs, entrepreneurs, academics, educators, professionals, and from a wide range of corporate, nonprofit, academic, small-business, and Fortune 100 organizations. If you responded, or are going to respond, thank you. The insights, anecdotes, and data have made this book stronger. The study continues, too, and you can join the survey at LisaBragg.com.

## Onward, Together

In Part 1 of the book, we'll uncover why we're hidden gems (people who truly have something special to offer but are overlooked or unnoticed) and the truth about why some of us stay this way. I'll tell you why this isn't all about *me, me, me,* and you'll understand that this isn't do-it-yourself—it's a do-it-together endeavor.

In Part 2, we'll explore actionable steps. We'll move forward with simple principles that will support your bragging and self-promotion efforts so you can increase your social currency, while also learning the mistakes to avoid. I'll share how you can aid those you lead, mentor, or champion in shedding their invisibility cloaks and how you can help them shine. Helping people move from invisible to visible increases their sense of belonging, which if you're a leader, say, means a healthier, more productive team. Executives who bring me into their organizations see my programs as a way to help their talent pipeline problems. As an added bonus, when you shine a light on others, it has a way of making you look even brighter.

Each chapter of the book ends with three types of actions so you can keep moving the work forward:

- **To Consider:** This activity encourages you to reflect on something or germinate ideas. We don't often take the time to reflect deeply about ourselves, but the insights we gain can cause action.

- **To Do:** I want you to have easy wins along the way. These will be things that you can do right now, quickly.

- **To Share:** There's so much in this book you can share. I've set up some ways in which you can spread your bragging rights to others.

We're living in times of transformative change. The old secrets, formulas, and recipes don't work. We were all sold on outdated advice. This book is *the* update. I know the journey from invisible to visible seems like one with many pitfalls, but I have a strategy for success that I want to share with you. I've used it with thousands of people, and it will help you navigate the process. You'll be inspired, but you'll also need to act. I'll talk about courage and depending on yourself, as well as tapping into all your seen and unseen allies to move forward further and faster. Those tiny steps of courage might feel uncomfortable, but you must keep coming back to take another step.

# PART ONE
# RECLAIMING BRAGGING RIGHTS

**FOR SOME, IT ROLLS OFF** the tongue as if they were born with it. For the rest of us, bragging and self-promotion is something we have to learn (or relearn). When well-meaning people say, "Just be more confident" or "Get out there and talk about yourself" or "Start doing social media," they have an understanding gap. It's not just an individualized solution to a social problem. In Part 1, we'll look at what's behind the culture that might let you through one door but, with its pressures and limitations, keep you stuck in that room until you become a load-bearing wall.

You may already be aware of the environment that pushes the ideas that you don't need validation, that you have to earn your spot, or that bragging and self-promotion are too risky for you. These challenges started long before we were born, but we must understand them today so we can move forward now.

# A Case for Bragging

AT THE pinnacle of being seen and heard, opportunities come to you. The people who know you help you even more. Those who don't know you hear about you and see you, even open doors you never thought were possible or simply hadn't considered. They partner with you to make this level of development easier and more secure, or they lead you to the next level of growth. I've had doors open for me. It's magic. It's fantastic. The opportunities have been both large and small but have led to other awesome things that have allowed me to share my mission. At the pinnacle, you're set up for the future, with social currency to spare, able to manage risks and help others. I've let the world know my value and how I am here to serve by helping people get more opportunities. But it wasn't always that way.

About ten years into the life of my company, MediaFace, I experienced a pivotal moment in my career. Surprisingly, it came in a nondescript manila envelope that had been delivered by regular mail. And things went quickly downhill. The envelope contained a thick file announcing legal action against my small company.

Regarding the work that led to the action, I had taken what I thought were the proper steps for a complicated business issue. The advice I got from legal experts wasn't wrong, but it wasn't airtight.

I handed the claim over to my lawyers, but curiosity got the better of me, so I looked up the lawyer who had filed the action to see why he would take this case. Two sentences on his website shook me. He liked to go after the reputation of companies and their principals, often using the media for maximum effect. A great tactic when you want people to settle fast.

I tried to tell myself I had no real reason to worry—the circumstances weren't newsworthy and really wouldn't make the lawyer's client look good. But in the moment, it was messy. I was on an emotional roller coaster. I took the legal action as an attack. Yes, a bruised ego was involved, but there was something more unsettling: I felt exposed. My inner good girl was rocked to her core, and impostor syndrome reverberated loudly in my mind.

I worried that this situation would sully my company's dealings with my high-profile corporate, government, and academic clients. I felt vulnerable, powerless, and frustrated because there was nothing I could do but leave things to the lawyers. I couldn't use my hard-work ethic to get out of it. I couldn't use my reputation or track record to get ahead of it. As I worked through why this was bothering me so deeply, I realized that if my business ever did fail, or if I wanted to walk away from it immediately, I wasn't well set up to go for other opportunities.

But after listening to P!nk on repeat and being my own dancing queen every morning in the kitchen to get going on my day, it hit me that I could do something. I could take control of my professional life in a way I hadn't before and create a safety net just in case anything ever happened again.

I had to build past my title and tell those who mattered to me why I, Lisa Bragg, was remarkable, in a way that would allow me to easily pivot. My company was already helping other companies' subject-matter experts be seen as thought leaders and visionaries. Individual leaders would ask me, "Well, how do I do this for myself too?" They saw the benefit of the work others were doing. This led me to consulting and advising on personal-professional strategies and plans for leaders, executives, and CEOs. These people believed they were being passed over because they weren't the loudest in the room. Politically, they needed to be subtle, but they ended up being invisible. They were mid- or late career and stuck, or they were at the top of their game but felt as if they were stalling and sometimes burning out. Some had lost the power their position had afforded them when they changed roles. I loved my work, but it took a threat to move me to be bolder and fully own my efforts, not the call of endless opportunities.

So why hadn't I done it before—that is, really worked in earnest to self-promote or share my value with the world? I had myriad excuses. Perhaps I was more concerned about being perceived as obnoxious or about the potential for feeling "icky" about actively self-promoting than I was with truly wanting to be visible. With wishful thinking, I thought that even though everyone was incredibly busy, they would somehow be sure to stop by my tiny corner of the world and see my contributions and accomplishments. I had yet to unpack the cultural and societal norms that had been overly prescribed to me. And I hadn't done the thinking to recast myself beyond any role or job path so that I was positioned for the future and not a product of the past.

## My Last Name *Is* Bragg

You'll have noticed my last name by now: Bragg.

It may come as a surprise to you that with a name like this, I've struggled to tell my stories, and some of that comes from a hang-up I had about my last name—which was originally a nickname for a brisk, lively, and cheerful person.

But perhaps you can imagine that as a teenager, I experienced a bit of teasing about my last name, some of which bordered on bullying.

We learn what we are meant to teach. I think that because of my last name, in my early teens I was keenly aware of the tangles and tripwires around talking about your successes. More than a few times, a public win at school would include the sneering comment, "Are you going to brag about it?" A win by someone else wouldn't garner even an eye roll. I used that pettiness as fuel but kept my personal bragging and self-promotion to a minimum. I realized that some people's success bothered other people in a way that didn't make sense.

Since those early days, I've extensively studied bragging and self-promotion, and I've also deeply considered the worry, fear, and shame we have inside ourselves as a result of standing out or even considering standing out. I know the frustration and burnout that comes from waiting for others to notice you and the corrosive effect that feeling invisible has on one's well-being. It's an extremely high price to pay. And regretting not taking the steps now to stand out, show up, and do the work you want to do—regretting not creating the opportunities for yourself you know you deserve—is worse.

## From Hidden to Daylight

This era of rapidly shifting ideals and incentives is altering our pathways as we walk. My hope is that you will be able to usher in the change you want to see and find others who will support you along the way. I want the world to know the awesomeness you bring so that you can make whatever size dent you wish to improve it. If not now, when? If not you, who?

If you weren't exhausted, concerned, or afraid, and if things were risk-free, what would you feel, think, do, and say about yourself? That's a challenging question so early in the book, so tuck it away to consider. But you do have a choice to make: Do you want to stand by and continue being hidden or to show up and act?

I want you to feel comfortable putting your work in the spotlight. I want you to feel so comfortable talking about your work as *success*, right out in the open, in the daylight. For all of us, I want bragging and self-promotion to be so common that both are expected, accepted, and nurtured. I want us to expect it of ourselves and encourage it in others.

Bragging shouldn't be special at all. In our work together, you don't have to covet the spotlight to be seen and heard. This isn't about fame and fortune. It's not just for the extremely magical or the extremely flawless—it's for all of us. It shouldn't be reserved for characters who are larger than life. An audience of one critical person can make all the difference.

Bragging is, however, still a bit of a rebellion, but it's a rebellion at the right time, and we will undertake it together. I am your ally. Reach out to me as you learn to brag. I'm at hello@lisabragg.com, or on social media I'm front and center as Lisa Bragg. Tag any comments with #BraggingRights and I'll find you.

If you weren't exhausted, concerned, or afraid, and if things were risk-free, what would you feel, think, do, and say about yourself?

Social constructs that determine who is valuable right now, our rules, and why there are limitations—all of this is made up. Another fake rule is that you must succeed by the time you are thirty-five. This book is entirely made up too. But it's made up of what I know works from my own experiences, clients, and research. Success can come at any time.

So, here's an easy win. You can start easing into bragging by sending me a note, either by direct messaging or public posting, that describes something you've accomplished. It can be something as significant or as inconsequential as you like, as long as it makes you proud.

## Language Matters

Before we go further, let's pause to consider the definition of a few terms, so that we are all using the same language.

**Brag.** When I use "brag" and all its derivatives, I mean talking about your successes and accomplishments in a positive way. It's brave and spirited, and it wants all people to shine. This definition is much closer to the semantic roots of the word.

In 1325, "brag" meant "proud; spirited, brave" and not boastful. In early modern English, it meant "brave, spirited." In Scandinavian sources, *braga* means "to flicker" (of the northern lights), along with "blaze, flash" and "to show off, display." German and Dutch equivalents mean "to shine and shimmer." The word also has connections to "challenge, defy."

Dictionaries define "bragging" as a means to talk about your successes with pride, and pride's meaning can range from "conceit" to "reasonable and justifiable self-respect." Philosopher Richard Taylor defined pride as "the justified love of oneself."

Let's go with that, knowing that the pursuit of bragging is not in singular self-interest but also for the sake of others.

**Self-aggrandizing.** Bragging is in opposition to self-aggrandizing. When we think of the negativity around talking about your successes, what we're actually thinking of is self-aggrandizing, which means "the act of making oneself more powerful, wealthy, or important, especially in a ruthless way." This is where the put-downs happen, the puffery, the "I'm better than you" attitude. The "ickiness" that so many report seeing online lives in the word "self-aggrandizement." When we see someone showing off "their" yacht when they are a guest in the harbor, that's a mild form of self-aggrandizing and one popularized on social media. Misalignment between what you believe to be true about a person and what they are portraying causes an internal kerfuffle.

**Modesty.** We're called to be modest far too frequently, to be unassuming and not "too" confident. Dictionaries like the word "modest," but the term is also a trap that too often refers to women's clothing or behavior. Author Maya Angelou disliked modesty. She told writer Dawn Reiss of *The Atlantic* that arrogance is denying one's own specialness—and denying the specialness of others. "You see, I have no patience with modesty," she said. "Modesty is a learned adaptation. It's stuck on like decals. As soon as life slams a modest person against the wall, that modesty will fall off faster than a G-string will fall off a stripper.

"Whenever I'm around some who is modest, I think, 'run like hell and all of fire,'" she said. "You don't want modesty, you want humility. Humility comes from inside out. It says someone was here before me and I'm here because I've been paid for. I have something to do and I will do that because I'm paying for someone else who has yet to come."

Modesty calls for us to deflect or dismiss praise and accomplishments. It calls for us to be smaller than we are, which in itself is a privilege, a social trap, that no one reading this book can allow themselves or others to fall into. When you are modest, you are passive. You deny the skills you have earned and the attributes you have been given. You deny others the right to learn from you and be served by you. When you say, "Oh, it was nothing," those of us in awe feel your achievement is unattainable to us mere mortals. Other people will take you at your word and think that it truly was nothing. Meanwhile, it was a superstar moment that should lead to more opportunities—but why would it? It was nothing...

If you're squirming right now because you're shy or an introvert, let me assure you that removing the mantle of modesty (false or not) doesn't mean you have to be a raging extrovert. Self-promotion is about being smart, not loud or bombastic; we're also doing this with purpose.

**Humility.** There is a large, loud call for more humility from leaders. You already have humility and probably don't need more of it. You are not arrogant. You are a good listener and already know that you don't know what you don't know. You can be ambitious and humble. These traits are not at odds.

**Reputation versus brand promise.** Your brand promise is about the future—the potential of you. Your brand promise is what people say about you when you're not in the room. It gives you a helping hand to the future. Your reputation is how people judge you for your past. People get opportunities based on their potential. Do people know your potential? Wouldn't it be great if other people were mind readers?

**You always market yourself to where you want to go, not where you've been.** Most people spend so much time shoring up their pasts that they're not showing up for the future.

**Professional brand.** I'm not partial to the word "brand," but it's part of the vernacular. Remember: first, you are a human having a human experience, talking to humans. Your professional brand helps you make strategic choices. It helps describe your identity in that it's the differentiated value you deliver. It's a dialogue between those you serve, including your clients, customers, and stakeholders. It's only valid if your audience on the receiving end of that value perceives it to be valuable. For example, a purse is a purse, it just carries your things, but add a particular label to it and the bag suddenly costs $60,000.

You can't hand your brand to someone to figure out for you. It's about how you want to show up in the world. It isn't about having a logo or website; it's about you at your core—your values, your personality, and what drives you. It's a combination of the passion you held when you started your career and the wisdom you now hold.

The term "personal brand" overlaps, but it is more connected with being a social media influencer or selling lifestyle products, so the term I use is "professional brand." It's just the preference of whom I want to attract with my work. That's part of *my* brand.

**Social currency.** Social currency is the value you build up through your interactions. It's a reservoir of influence, connections, power, status, trust, authority, and goodwill that helps you close the opportunity gap. When you make a mistake, it can be lessened.

Often, social currency is associated with social media, but my use of the term extends beyond those platforms. You can no longer separate online and in person. Your social currency flows between being in person and being online.

"What the science is telling us is that it's important to signal to others what makes you a credible, knowledgeable authority before you make your influence attempt."

**ROBERT CIALDINI**

**Social proof.** Social proof establishes your credibility in your office, throughout your company, and in your industry, nationally or globally. Social proof helps people verify you are what and who you say you are. In the past, social proof might have been given through a letter of introduction or a call made on your behalf, but with our networks expanding and our constant online presence now, social proof has a wider range. It includes anything that can show and tell your awesomeness, such as podcasts, articles, testimonials, media appearances, and awards. It's your brag book out in the world and on display. It's about your performance, experience, achievements, wisdom, and skills. Your social proof speaks for you and does the heavy lifting of bragging when you're not around.

Social proof helps draw people to you and validates you when someone is looking for someone just like you. It's a reference that you are established and credible, and that you walk the talk. Your social proof satisfies people's curiosity and allows them to make a trust leap much quicker when it aligns with what they need. For example, if someone in the media sees that you have media experience, they'll be quicker to contact you when they need to. If you've successfully worked on massive accounts for clients, they'll feel confident in recommending you, but your self-promoted experience also allows potential clients to come to a decision about you quicker than they might otherwise. There are many ways to establish social proof, including some quick tips to come, but you can consider business credentials, social media shares, media appearances, internal newsletters, awards, and partnerships with people who already have credibility. External proof is stronger than an award you've given yourself.

**Self-promotion.** Self-promotion is the strategy behind getting people to notice what you want them to see—your brag-worthy points. How you execute self-promotion will change depending on the avenues available to you and the tactics best suited to your audience. It includes tactics you would use to get your messages out into the world (e.g., through video, e-learning, speaking, association newsletters, awards). Self-promotion is different from bragging in that bragging is your hook; it's about communicating the success you want your self-promotion efforts to support.

**Bragging rights.** "Bragging rights" is a positive and celebratory term. One dictionary defines it as "the opportunity to speak proudly because you have done something impressive." Who gets to say what is "impressive"? I'm giving you permission right now: you do. Your bragging rights are "a good reason to talk with pride about something you have done."

"Bragging rights" also means acknowledging that some people may need help speaking up about themselves and their work. As humans, we're all on the same team. We're all remarkable, and each of us should have the right to share what makes us special without the concern of penalty.

At the start of some programs I conduct, some people believe they're at a deficit with self-promotion because they don't have a tangible product to sell. But this isn't about selling your products or yourself; self-promotion is about sharing your ideas and vision. The goal is to have people lean in and want to know more.

## Self-Promotion Is Not about Product

My friend Michelle Watson owns Michi, a beautiful activewear clothing brand. She's a walking billboard in person, but she also shows her healthy lifestyle through her personal social media by posting photos of her adventures in the woods or rappelling down a cliff. She's also actively self-promoting offline, encouraging people to move their bodies and think about wellness, reinforcing what she values and cares about beyond her product. Because she actually lives her talk out loud, she's one of my go-to people I recommend to those who want to talk about fitness. Self-promotion is not about the brand you work for, even if it is your own company.

Mita Mallick is great at self-promoting without a product. Her goal isn't to sell anything, nor is she a consultant or coach. She gets her paycheck as head of inclusion, equity, and impact from a corporation. She's building her professional brand across several platforms and using tactics such as short posts on social media, articles in widely read publications such as *Harvard Business Review* and *Cosmopolitan*, and podcast episodes for LinkedIn. She has won awards. This has taken time to build up, but she's doing it to reinforce that she is a corporate change-maker. It's also helping her build social proof for her future endeavors. Her pillars demonstrate how inclusion is a driver of business, leadership lessons, and parenting. You'll learn more about Mallick later in the book.

## ••• Bragging Right •••

Bragging is about your future—tomorrow, next year, and ten years from now. The time to do it is now. There's an urgency with this work. You have a higher aspiration that needs to be seen, heard, and shared so you can get the opportunities you deserve. Today's work will position you or your legacy well into the future.

It's time to normalize—for everyone—talking about our success.

**To Consider:** Think about the compliments you've received lately. Compliments are gold. Spend ten minutes looking for emails or social posts in which someone has complimented you. What's one compliment you really should have received but didn't? Give it to yourself right now. Write it down. When you receive a compliment, don't deflect it. Look the person in the eye, simply thank them, and leave it at that. If you're too uncomfortable with that step, you can add something like, "I learned a lot through the experience."

**To Do:** Start a brag book. This is a place to write down the brags others make about you and that you identify for yourself. Record them in a folder, journal, or document. Don't wait until you need them. Information goes missing on servers all the time. Print out, download—just save those kudos today.

**To Share:** Reach out to two people to give them a genuine compliment. Make one public and one private. Appreciate what they've done for you or others. You don't have to know someone to send a compliment. Giving genuine praise is a great way to start to be seen. It must be honest, from the heart.

# 2

# A Legacy of Hiding

HUMANS COULDN'T run a four-minute mile. "Informed observers" said that no one could do it. It was impossible. Even so, for years, people put in a dedicated effort to best that time. Then in 1954, Roger Bannister did it. His record lasted just forty-six days. Four more people achieved it soon afterward. So what changed? We didn't suddenly all grow faster feet. A mental model adapted. Bannister did it, which meant it was possible. He transformed what was possible. Humans could then run a four-minute mile. But change doesn't happen in a straight line.

## The Legacy of Bragging

A long, long time ago, we had to talk openly and vigorously about our wins and successes as well as our failures and inadequacies. We passed down our legends and lore so that the species could thrive. Remember, "brag" used to be defined as "spirited, brave, and proud." In our small, nomadic groups, we were known. There was kinship, and survival meant being part of a collective.

When we moved into coalitions with single rulers, an individual's success was the ruler's success. Most would not want to stick their necks out too far, but status levels developed as communities grew larger. It was an agrarian way of life, where a person could be a skilled worker doing piecemeal work in collaboration with others, but 90 percent of people worked in farming. A person's strengths and weaknesses were in plain sight.

The industrial era bequeathed many of the norms and expectations of modesty that still hold today. People moved from small towns to commercial areas of concentrated factories, searching for steady income. Some came with families, others alone. The complexity of work required new hierarchies. The organism of factory work demanded a high level of cooperation and subordination. Opportunities were limited and people were plenty, so by and large, they did as they were told.

Novelist Charles Dickens made a career writing about the inhumanity of such industrialized systems and urban life. As the industrial revolution took hold, systems developed such that those in charge saw humans as simply cogs in the machine. Workers were owed only their wages for the previous week's work. If the owners and managers didn't have to think about, worry about, or consider their employees, then they could make more profit. Schools were set up to train people for factory life.

Of course, this is now a well-outdated model, but its legacy affects organizational structure even today. And although some countries remain in an industrial era, globalization and the new economy are rapidly changing the world of work. We cannot project what happens next from old leadership books or knowledge. As novelist William Gibson said, "The future is already here—it's just not very evenly distributed."

We remain stuck in the stories and norms of the past while other parts of this world change so quickly, we can't see the changes as they're happening. We're well beyond the factory era—the first and second industrial eras stretched from the 1700s to 1870 and even into the period that came after, in the 1960s, the digital revolution. We're now into the "fourth revolution," which started around 2009, and already quickly sliding into the fifth. These technological changes will fundamentally alter how we live, work, and relate to one another.

When this slide into the next era will happen we can't know, but in the meantime, thinking now that we're in the "imagination age" or "intelligence economy" will serve you. Think brain power over physical power or natural resources. This knowledge-based economy means that creativity, stewardship, social cohesion, and collaboration are critical. If you can imagine it, design it, and execute it, then you'll lead the future. You must create it, though—you can't wait for it. (Just like Bannister running the miracle mile.)

## No Such Thing as Irrelevant

It's okay that you feel lost or out of place. You face challenges that didn't exist before. Our communities used to be built in, not sought after. We're no longer competing in our backyards; we're growing markets, and it can be done almost anywhere in the world. We're working with people who aren't in the next cubicle over anymore—they're across the country or the globe. We're becoming more transient, changing not only jobs and companies but also industries and sectors, going from academia to corporate, from entrepreneur to NGO to government. You might be self-employed, freelance, or employed and working remotely. More and more people have portfolio careers—they work on several unrelated projects that require a range of skills.

Rather than building a résumé of work at one place for thirty-plus years, many are building a portfolio of experiences that connect to and prepare them for the future.

Dorie Clark is an expert in this type of work. She's a bestselling author and regular contributor to business magazines, including *Harvard Business Review*. Clark has a portfolio career and is not only the "expert's expert" and a professor, but she's also in an entirely different field, as a theatrical lyricist. In a conversation with me, Clark talked about the relative ease of spring-boarding into an additional pursuit because of the "halo effect." In the same way that actors or business leaders get elected as politicians, if you're perceived as good in one area, people will generalize and believe your skills are transferable to another. While musical theater might not be in your future, when people start to recognize the value of your work because you've shown it to them, they will give you the benefit of the doubt or be more willing to offer advanced credibility when you do something different.

The bottom line: you are not locked into one path.

## If You Can See It, You Can Be It

Fire, the wheel, electricity, and automation changed the story for past generations. Our current tools are now maturing. We no longer disseminate information in a show-and-tell manner solely controlled by a few old gatekeepers, and we've moved past the early Internet's "look what I can do, watch me world" attitude of self-promotion to a "join me" frame of mind. Our current and quickly forthcoming technology engenders collaboration and connection across vast distances. *For you to succeed in this new environment, you must see yourself in the world.*

Do we wait to change society or learn to navigate society as it is? We do both. We change the norms and we celebrate those who succeed.

Hollywood knows how powerful it is in setting a narrative (true or not) for many worldwide. Geena Davis, an actor who starred in *Thelma & Louise*, *A League of Their Own*, and many more movies, found that when she hit a certain age—forty—the quality roles dried up. She already knew that older women weren't being represented, and she wanted to know how widespread the problem was, on-screen and off, and what effect it had on society. The Geena Davis Institute on Gender in Media team coined "the Scully Effect" to describe how movie and TV show characters inspire behavior changes in the real world. Dana Scully, played by Gillian Anderson, is the female lead character of the 1990s hit TV show *The X-Files*. The team found that women who watched the science-fiction series regularly were 50 percent more likely to start careers in STEM (science, technology, engineering, math). Typically, these fields have been overwhelmingly filled by men.

If you can see it, you can be it.

How would you feel if you had inspired one of the people who now inspire the world? America Ferrera wanted to be an actor from the time she was nine years old, and in her twenties, she finally made it big with *Ugly Betty*. It was a smash-hit US comedy-drama based on the titular protagonist, Betty Suarez. Betty was a quirky, tenacious, hardworking young woman with a unique fashion sense, who got a job at a fashion magazine as an executive assistant but wanted to be a writer. The show was nominated for eleven Emmys in its first year.

In Ferrera's 2019 TED Talk, "Identity Is a Superpower—Not an Obstacle," she said,

> It's been twelve years since I became the first and only Latina to ever win an Emmy in a lead category. That is not a point of pride. That is a point of deep frustration. Not because awards prove

our worth, but because who we see thriving teaches us how to see ourselves, how to think about our own value, how to dream about our futures.

And anytime I begin to doubt that, I remember that there was a little girl living in the Swat Valley of Pakistan. And somehow, she got her hands on some DVDs of an American television show in which she saw her own dream of becoming a writer reflected. In her autobiography, Malala wrote, "I had become interested in journalism after seeing how my own words could make a difference and also from watching the *Ugly Betty* DVDs about life at an American magazine."

Ferrera uses her success to campaign for more humanity and justice. More and more women are claiming the narrative in Hollywood and popular media. We're seeing more women collaborate with others to tell stories that would not have been told even in the recent past. In the past, those women would have been competing against each other for a seat at the table. Now, through self-promotion and bragging rights, they can make their own table, and others are coming to it.

## Undervaluing Ourselves to Manage Expectations

Lisa Mattam, a former pharmaceutical executive, now owns an international beauty line of ayurvedic products. In a podcast interview, I asked her about a time she wished she had been bolder. Her response was that she continually underestimates herself and she feels she does it to manage expectations. She told me about a colleague who boasts about how awesome his products are, about his clients, and his prospects. He has no issues with saying that he's the best and nothing is going to hold him back. Mattam said, "And then one day, he happened to not say the exact number, but he suggested how much money the business was making a month. And I almost fell off my chair because I was like, 'Really?' Not because it wasn't good, but because I thought it was so much bigger than it was."

That reveal gave Mattam a bigger window into how she plays the game. She realized that she uses words, consistently and sometimes unknowingly, that diminish her capacity. "I'd tell you in a conversation that I work with a small agency. I don't need to qualify that. I work with an agency," she said. "I use language that minimizes things, and I don't do it with intent. I think I do it sometimes because I feel like I have to manage expectations. I worry that someone will say, 'Well, you're only this big or you're only this'—and it's all constructed in my head. So I wish I was bolder, every day, because in that boldness is where greatness is going to live."

Mattam is not alone in her experiences. Although many of us want to put ourselves out there, we hesitate. We stay with what feels safe and comfortable. We remain within moral norms dictated by social groups; the culture we consume, including stories shared in media and on social media (including your company's intranet or the gossip grapevine); and those learned and reinforced in institutions and by authority figures. Leaders set norms and they can also be set by others we work closely with. Norms tell us what people want us to do and what they think we should and shouldn't do. We often fear the real or perceived backlash from stepping outside the norm. Often, cultural norms set by those in power are based on myths that, when times change, linger longer than is helpful. Western culture has many outdated myths worthy of question.

## Myth: Cream Rises to the Top

One such myth is the idiom that cream rises to the top. This "magical milk" saying suggests that if you're good, you'll rise to the top. However, a US survey by the Society for Human Resource Management conducted in 2020 found that 84 percent of workers said their poorly trained managers create a lot of unnecessary work and stress. This provides evidence that the above expression is not only outdated but incorrect.

## Myth: If You Wait for It, You Will Be Chosen

The prevailing myth here is that if we wait for our big moment, somehow, we'll be plucked out of obscurity and chosen for a more desirable role. This kind of fantasy is a distraction from making your own luck.

In 1984, a rock and roll legend nicknamed "The Boss" plucked a young woman out of a stadium crowd to dance on stage with him. That young woman went on to star in a famous show that most people have heard of—*Friends*. It was long believed that Courteney Cox had been extremely lucky, just in the right place at the right time.

But the truth is, Cox was already an actor who had starred in commercials and a soap opera. While "dancing in the dark" with Bruce Springsteen likely did help her career, Cox wasn't a random hidden gem dancing in the crowd. She was an actor who had auditioned for Springsteen's music video, for the role of the fan who couldn't believe she'd been plucked from obscurity by this legend. But in real life, she was putting herself out there, working to be picked.

## Myth: Wait Your Turn

Marie called me, searing-hot mad. She was frustrated that one of her competitors, a newcomer to the industry, had been recently

"Each of us is very special, very singular, carrying weight. I matter. I would like to open the window tonight and yell that outside. I matter."

DOROTHEA LYNCH

singled out for magazine features. Sean was a younger, new-style player who'd bought someone else's business. Marie was floored when he won the prestigious award she'd had her heart set on for more than thirty years in the industry; she thought she should have won. Before this, the award had been an honor bestowed on people who had tenure with a good track record, including a strong book of business and employee engagement.

The unofficial rules of the past had been to show up, pay your dues, and wait your turn. Marie had learned them when she joined the industry at a younger age than Sean. But when the officials chose Sean, they said, "It is refreshing to have young people join the win."

There's no room for feeling entitled, as Marie did. She made a few calls and learned that Sean had been actively campaigning for the award by talking to key members. I pointed out that he had been showing up strategically online and in association media.

He wasn't going to follow the norms that had been set out. He wasn't in the "go along to get along" frame of mind. He saw the easy room for disruption to get the award he wanted, and the judges agreed. At the formal annual gala, there was a standing ovation for Sean, who picked up his award—in flip-flops.

## Myth: Your Work Speaks for Itself

While I appreciate much of the work of academic and author Adam Grant, this statement and its continual perpetuation frustrates me: "Bragging about yourself violates norms of modesty and politeness—and if you were really competent, your work would speak for itself."

He wrote that in 2013, but quite a bit has happened in the years since, including the COVID-19 pandemic, #MeToo, the Black Lives Matter movement, more social media platforms, and changes to modesty norms. In 2020, I had an opportunity to ask Grant if he still stood by his comment—specifically if women, especially Indigenous, Black, or other women of color, now need to brag and self-promote to get ahead. He said, "The answer is complex," but he stood by his comment because according to the research, the risk and backlash to women who brag and self-promote is too great.

Let's consider that for a moment. Yes, there are risks, and the backlash potential is real. I'll delve into both later in this book, but although Grant's quote may contain grains of truth, the prolificacy of his quote and what that suggests has implications for bragging. Who is setting the modesty rules? Who is setting the competency bar? What comes first: social change or research? What if you don't have access to power? What if you're not part of the dominant culture?

Lola Akinmade Åkerström is an author and award-winning photographer. She has an international lens as a citizen of Nigeria, the US, and now Sweden. She works as a travel photographer and has been featured in *National Geographic* and on BBC, CNN, and elsewhere. She often gives speeches about how she got her status. Her portfolio is on par with those of her high-level peers, but in conversation she told me that when some audiences see a woman behind the photos, it clashes with their perception, and her work suddenly becomes "not good enough." There's also a cultural aspect that needs to be unpacked, she said, "so when people say, 'Oh, the work should speak for itself,' who is the work talking to? If there is a Black artist creating amazing Afrocentric art, that is fantastic, but because it doesn't appeal to a white audience, then they're like, well, the work is not for me. It's not that great; it's a matter of personal taste. It's super-subjective."

Rules and the status quo aren't set in stone. The notion that we shouldn't talk about our accomplishments with pride because it isn't polite limits our human potential, and it keeps power limited to the old gatekeepers. Do we wait to change society or learn to navigate society as it is? My answer to that conundrum is: we do both. We push to change the norms and we celebrate those who succeed. We're having the tough conversations about what's going wrong, but we're struggling to have the conversations that should be easy—about our successes, accomplishments, experiences, and performance. It's an essential exchange in the world of work—to be seen and heard and to see others.

## Myth: Women of a Certain Age Are Invisible

There's also the myth that women become invisible once they reach a certain age. (You can pick an age. Hollywood used to say thirty, Geena Davis found it was forty...) Not that long ago, if you weren't married by twenty-five, you were considered a spinster, which was usually a villainized single woman. Western culture excessively scrutinizes women as they age, and year by year erases their influence. The reality is that we develop our life's work over time; then we need to reinterpret it in later stages.

Bonnie Marcus has studied this extensively. In her book, *Not Done Yet! How Women Over 50 Regain Their Confidence and Claim Workplace Power*, she notes that gendered ageism is indeed real, and it has a negative effect not only on women in general but also, specifically, on professional women and their career trajectories. We all face the sense of feeling invisible, unseen, and unknown as we age. It just happens much earlier for women, and Bonnie says it is because "of the importance placed on our looks." You shouldn't be invisible as a human. No matter your gender, mindset is critical. Be visible, most importantly to yourself. You must stay in the game and continually produce regardless of age.

## ••• Bragging Right •••

Institutions, systems, and our cultures haven't been set up for everyone to win. There's a need to detangle societal messages. More of us need to grab the tools and tell our own stories so that our imagination and intelligence disrupt the myths. Your social currency matters now more than it ever has for making the today and tomorrow you want.

**To Consider:** Think about what myths or old concepts you hold on to that are no longer serving you. How might you reframe them?

**To Do (a):** Identify anything that stops you from bragging. Here are some possibilities:

- You may be dismissing your successes by not keeping track or by downplaying your strengths.
- The people surrounding you may not want to celebrate success.
- You might be standing in your way.

**To Do (b):** Spend fifteen minutes researching people who appear to be achieving something you admire. Look outside your company, industry, and country. What is it you admire? What can you glean from what they have shared? What can you learn from them that can benefit you? Think about the Scully Effect. Is there a fictional character who has inspired you? What were her traits? What was the story?

**To Share:** Connect with someone who has inspired you to reach outside your comfort zone and tell them they did so. Gratitude is a great way to develop and enhance connections.

# 3

# How Power Plays In

RITA, WHO was new to a financial firm where I was mentoring, lamented that she left her previous firm where she had been promised a director job because her boss, Krish, had moved up and on. When he resigned, Rita says, he forgot his "implied" promise to bring her up the company ranks. She had spent so much time making Krish look good and hadn't spent time building her own social capital. She belatedly realized that he hadn't spread any goodwill about her. Rita decided to start fresh at a new company rather than rebuild under a new leader.

During a group mentoring session with her new team, it became clear, though, that Rita hadn't learned her lesson. She thought it was just Krish and it wouldn't happen again. She believed her work "would speak for itself" or that Eleanor (her new VP) would help her move up. I asked her to think about it this way: What if Eleanor won the lottery? But before Rita could respond, Eleanor quickly quipped, "Oh, no, Rita, you have to do this yourself. Your career is your responsibility." Applause, applause. Eleanor didn't want that kind of power over Rita's career.

Rita's example demonstrates that you cannot simply play by the old rules and expect to win. Consider this from Carol Dweck, a Stanford psychology professor and author of *Mindset: The*

*New Psychology of Success*: "If life were one long grade school, women would be the undisputed rulers of the world." Those rules you were so good at following and that are wired into your brain don't continue in most organizations.

Advancement based on your capabilities and merits (in other words, meritocracy) and having nothing to do with your family, wealth, social standing, or other aspects of your identity (for example, your gender, skin color, ability status, sexual orientation) sounds ideal. But that's not how things currently work. Unless they are making a sincere and effective effort toward diversity, equity, and inclusion, companies that hold meritocracy as a core value tend to look for people who are most like those already there and most worthy of merit. Meritocracy is subjective, artificial, and incomplete.

The concept that those at the top deserve to be there has a shadow side: the belief that those at the bottom also deserve to be there. But there are far too many inept leaders high on charisma and low on delivery. Meritocracy is a faulty system. For most of us, however, partnering, community, and interpersonal skills are important for creating opportunities.

## Hemmed In

Women know they need to brag and self-promote as part of the modern and future workforce, but they face real and suggested penalties if they do. In the Bragging Rights survey, 60 percent of respondents felt that women are penalized socially for talking about their success.

Mary Ann Sieghart, author of *The Authority Gap*, was a London-based journalist for high-profile publications for more than twenty years. She became the target of a recurring satirical magazine with the parody column "Mary Ann Bighead." As she told me in an interview, while she tried to laugh along, the experience was painful, primarily since the tabloid also targeted her daughters, who were still in school. She said, "I thought it was unfair because I'm not particularly self-promoting. I try to be as confident as my male colleagues because, frankly, in the highly competitive world of newspaper journalism, you don't get anywhere if you're not as confident as your male colleagues. But merely by behaving as if I had as much right to be in the room as they did was interpreted as me being a big head, which I wasn't, I didn't think. Certainly, no more than any of my colleagues, probably less than most of the men."

As a social psychologist at Columbia Business School, Adam Galinsky has investigated this double bind for more than twenty years. His research has shown that, at the core, the issue is one of power, not gender. Those with less privilege in the social hierarchy, such as women, racialized communities, people of lower social classes, and people in lower-ranking positions in organizations, are prescribed narrower ranges of acceptable behavior.

Galinsky interviewed thousands of people to understand the dilemma of speaking up. "I've come to recognize that each of us have [sic] something called a range of acceptable behavior. And this range of acceptable behavior is [that] when we stay within our range we're rewarded, and when we step outside that range, we get punished in a variety of ways. We get dismissed or demeaned or even ostracized or we lose that raise or that promotion or that deal." A person's range of acceptable behavior isn't fixed. It is based on context.

People in power have a very wide range of acceptable behavior. However, if you don't have power, if you misread a situation, people may respond with an attitude as if to say, "Who do you think you are?" which is designed to keep people "in their place."

In times past, the power gap meant we stayed quiet about our work around the people who could be our champions. But we are in a new era.

As Sieghart rightly said to me, "It's not women we need to fix. It's how we all perceive and react to and interact with women that we need to fix. The problem is how we react to women when they start being confident and assertive or promoting themselves."

In other words, we need to extend the range of acceptable behavior. Influential people need to lead by example and ensure everyone shares their successes, especially women and other less privileged groups. This will start to shift culture in organizations and more broadly.

We also need facilitators, rather than obstructors, to support women as they work toward the next stage in their careers. Personal branding expert Stefan Scheidt defines facilitators as people who show others how to advance. The problem, he says, is that even if we have facilitators as we're starting out, "later, we have obstructors."

Obstructors are the colleagues and immediate superiors who are worried about the risk, feel envy or skepticism, or fear the loss of their reputation. (These are the people who leave you with empty promises.) Just as it sounds, they're the people who will stand in your way. Scheidt found that top managers tend to say obstructors are a fact of life. But we can look for and curate facilitators both organizationally and personally.

## Status Roles

I was a long-time fan of TED Talks. So when the licenses came up to host independent TEDx Talks in 2009, I jumped at the chance to bring it to Canada as an executive producer and host. At that time, we had to practically beg people to speak. No one wanted to do it because TED simply didn't have the status yet.

Now, having a TEDx Talk is highly coveted. People fly all over the world to be on one of the stages of these independently run, volunteer-organized events. It is a status symbol. Appearing on the main stage at a full TED conference is next level—and I got there.

At a TEDWomen conference, the organizers asked for people to submit a one-minute talk to give on the TED stage. I jumped at the chance to do it and was chosen. My 127-word speech was the genesis for this book. Being selected by the TED committee gave me the chance to connect with others in a new way. People in the audience approached me after my talk to find out more about me, to tell me their stories, and to encourage me to write a book or talk to their groups. Those connections have been extremely helpful in writing this book and in amplifying it so that I reach more audiences.

Consciously or unconsciously, most people consider whether they will gain or lose status when making decisions, although they're usually more interested in maintaining status than gaining it. Status is contextual. Sometimes a person has high status, sometimes low, and sometimes that status extends only to a tiny group (like people who held a TEDx license in 2009—we thought it was high status, but others didn't see the value).

While status changes for individuals, guardians of the status quo are at work. They want to retain power. They say, "Don't rock the boat," "Let your work speak for itself," "Keep your head down and do good work," and "No, we've never done it like that before." These types of statements reinforce who is entitled to what and when. How do these guardians benefit from maintaining the status quo? They create an "otherness" when people move up in status, instead of status being fluid.

Many of us have been following an outdated model: you can't win unless you've already won or are close to the winners. In times past, the power gap meant we stayed quiet about our work around the people who could be our champions. But we are in a new era. Bragging and self-promotion create social currency that we must collect and use.

## Stolen Credit

A whopping 77 percent of respondents to the Bragging Rights survey said that someone else had taken credit for their work—and not an "I also contributed to this piece of work" kind of credit. This was someone else lifting a metaphorical folder out of someone's done tray and presenting the contents as their work.

For women, the phenomenon of misplaced credit is called the Matilda Effect. Coined by Margaret Rossiter in 1993, the phrase refers to women who made significant contributions to science but were written out of the history books and denied awards and recognition in their lifetime. Women already face systemic bias and are often ignored or denied credit, while another person seizes or is given credit. People will grab and claim credit if it is left lying around. That's why the idea of waiting for other people to credit you or wait to be acknowledged is antiquated and fraught with the old status quo.

This includes work on teams. We have this nice notion that there isn't an "I" in teams. But being part of a successful team doesn't automatically mean we will earn and receive credit. It is critical to our future opportunities to claim credit for our work. Albert-László Barabási is a physicist who works on network theory, focusing on understanding complex systems. He analyzed how credit flows: "While team success requires diversity and balance, a single individual will receive credit for the group's achievements." Who gets credit has nothing to do with who did the work. Credit is based on perception. "And so," he says, "we put this one under the data microscope to figure out how do people decide about work credit. The mechanism is relatively simple, and it's very predictable and quantifiable. Typically, the credit goes to the individual, independent of how much he or she did on that particular team, whose line of work much closely fits with what the team has accomplished." Those who have garnered credit in the past will get the credit again, no matter how little work they did on a project or how much more others did on it. If someone just picked up the coffee but was team hero last time, they'll be seen as team hero again.

## Unconscious Bias

Part of what we need to overcome in order to normalize bragging about our work relates to unconscious bias and internalized sexism. If you think a woman shouldn't be talking about her work in a way that frames it as important and successful, you may have unwittingly accepted limiting ideas.

Kristen Pressner is global head of human resources at a multinational firm, supporting more than 35,000 people. One day, two team members—a man and a woman—asked her to look at their compensation. A few days later, while she was researching unconscious bias, she realized that she'd had two very different reactions to the same request. She had seen the man as the "provider" but hadn't seen the woman the same way. Yet Pressner's husband is a stay-at-home dad, and she is the sole provider for her family. "Particularly shocking to me was I'd always thought that you could only have a bias against someone who was different [from] you," she said. "So it really struck me to discover, to realize, we can have a bias against exactly what we are."

"We hold people responsible for the arc of their destiny."

ALAIN DE BOTTON

Pressner decided to test herself by flipping her perspectives. This is a devil's advocate position you can try with yourself. In her TEDxBasel Talk, she says, "Mentally flip whoever you're dealing with for someone else, to test yourself." To give an example, she showed a picture of a woman next to a picture of a man. Under the woman were the words "leader," "provider," "assertive," "strong," and "driven." Under the man were the words "supportive," "emotional," "helpful," "sensitive," and "fragile." She had flipped the photos. The audience laughed, and she asked them if the result felt off. "If it feels weird," she said, "you may want to check yourself."

### ••• Bragging Right •••

Fear of backlash for stepping out of the norm tends to hold people back. Cultures, within organizations and more broadly, need to change so that everyone feels comfortable claiming what is rightfully theirs. When we take pride in ourselves, our mental health benefits, so give yourself that pat on the back.

**To Consider:** How does your work benefit your team or wider stakeholders? Is it your skills, knowledge, or experience? Do you hold a group together? Provide mentorship? Teach and train?

**To Do:** Identify who you want to influence. Consider the other person's perspective. Perspective-taking is helpful when you're negotiating or wanting to influence an outcome. Use these priming questions to practice, writing in point form for about a minute in response to each question:

- What does the person think about themselves?
- What does the person think about you?

- What do you think about the person?
- What do you think about yourself?

**To Share:** Teach others Pressner's "Flip It to Test It" method to help more people get in the habit of "catching themselves" in decision making. Make it common to say, "Should we flip it to test it?" Mentally flip the identity of whomever you're dealing with for someone else, to test yourself. For example, if you think you shouldn't brag, mentally flip it. Would you think it's okay coming from someone else, someone who wasn't like you, to talk about their success? If your perspective looks, sounds, or feels weird, you may have an unconscious bias.

# 4

# How We Are at Odds

SAWUBONA IS a Zulu greeting that means "I see you" and "we see you," though it doesn't have a direct English translation. Roche Mamabolo, who runs an innovation and entrepreneurship center in South Africa, explains the meaning: "*Sawubona*, we see you, not simply your physical appearance, of course, but also your hopes, your fears, your dreams, your background, and the path you plan to take in the future." This word means we see and recognize people as human beings with emotions and ideas. You are more important than you realize. Every single person is important and needs to be seen. No one is above another. It means that we are all chosen.

And yet, we are at odds. What we want and need to do to make our mark isn't aligned with how many of us were raised. What should be the easiest thing, talking about our work in a way that frames its success, is one of the hardest acts for so many of us.

Our cultural lens affects how we speak up for ourselves. Initially, I thought the reluctance to self-promote was a Canadian thing. I'm going to lean in heavily on a stereotype about Canadians, and these statements don't apply to everyone. But there is a common myth that as Canadians, we want to be agreeable and likeable. We're known for apologizing when things are socially awkward. We're encouraged to give others the floor and not make it about ourselves.

But as I started talking about bragging and self-promotion to people worldwide, the reaction was the same. People in the East, West, North, and South from a wide variety of backgrounds said, "Well, that's me, that's my culture too." As you do when you're in a line at a conference, I started talking with an older woman and found out about the fantastic business she had built and sold, and the boards she currently sits on. She was fascinating. When we shuffled forward in line and the conversation turned to me, I thought, *There's no way this woman from New York would be interested in my premise.* So I said, "This might not be for you, but you know how we're taught to be good girls, put our heads down, do good work, and then eventually someone will notice us? My book is to move us beyond that so that we can brag about our work and get more opportunities." I paused. She chuckled and said, "Honey, I'm Catholic—*of course* that book is for me."

We all have cultural, societal, and institutional parameters. In the (admittedly surface-level) look at a few different cultural lenses on bragging, you might recognize cultural limits and nuances you ascribe to. Being able to label these and identify our own and others' current "zone of appropriateness" is an advantage. The rules are changing as we blend more in this peer-to-peer, knowledge-based economy. You'll have an advantage if you navigate away from what holds you back.

## The Law of Jante

There are hidden rules in Scandinavian countries. Don't be surprised if someone pulls the metaphorical microphone away from you. You likely broke one or more of the laws of *Janteloven* (the Law of Jante), a code of conduct initially created in fiction and that governs life in those countries. There are ten rules. Here's a selection:

- You shall not believe you are anything.
- You shall not believe you are good for anything.
- You shall not believe anyone cares about you.
- You shall not believe you can teach us anything.

**The Law of Jante sets cultural norms.** The rules classify the role of the individual within the collective but don't offer guidelines for a group. It's about how *you* fit into the group. These unofficial rules were first set out in Danish-born Norwegian writer Aksel Sandemose's 1933 novel *En flyktning krysser sitt spor* (*A Fugitive Crosses His Tracks*). The highly influential book was a satire set in a fictional small town, with the lead character delving into his memories of growing up, being raised by a factory worker, and the struggle to make ends meet. A "who do you think you are?" societal attitude had been in place long before the book, but the novel entrenched the thinking and consideration of these unspoken rules for generations.

Talking about individualism and collectivism is complicated. Some see rules like these as keeping people modest. Others see them as a form of social control to suppress the masses. Nowadays, with the globally connected world, young people especially are rebelling against the Law of Jante. In Norway, they made a grave for it.

The Law of Jante, however, is so ingrained in the social fabric and deep in everyone's wiring that it might not go away. Nigerian photographer Lola Akinmade Åkerström, mentioned earlier, made her home in Stockholm, Sweden, and has written several books, including LAGOM: *The Swedish Secret of Living Well*. Akinmade Åkerström defines Lagom essentially to mean making optimal decisions. During our interview, she explained to me that both the laws of Lagom and Jante embody an "ethos that [tries] to remove stress. Whereas Lagom wants you to live your best life, Jante wants people to be average—so in a group setting, because my Lagom is not your Lagom, it's causing stress. So it's trying to keep everybody from living [their] best life. Don't shine too much because you're stressing me. It changes depending on if you're with people of similar backgrounds—then they'll talk more freely and brag."

Of Nigeria, Akinmade Åkerström said, in contrast, "Nigerians are really proud, and I think where they attach pride to [is] respect and culture. They tend to brag in kind of shrouded ways: 'Oh, my daughter just got her master's.' The other person says, 'Oh, that's wonderful. God bless her... you know, maybe God bless her to get a PhD, like my daughter.' It's a kind of one-upmanship."

## It's in the Air

In Japan, bragging and self-promotion are frowned upon. In this very collectivist culture, they have the saying, "A nail sticking out gets hammered down." There's also an extremely high degree of humility engrained in women. But the panel of Japanese women I interviewed through an interpreter thought the culture of bragging was slowly changing. Ayumi Nishimura, who works at Ernst & Young, told me that typically bragging can "never come from their mouths, but they can write it. If you say it, you'll lose popularity."

The panel of women also included Erika Hirose, a mother of two who works as a homemaker; Akane Takahashi, a mother of one who is a former Morgan Stanley employee; and Harumi Gondo, who is Japanese American and who founded

What should be the easiest thing, talking about our work in a way that frames its success, is one of the hardest acts for so many of us.

a Myers–Briggs personality type community in Japan. Collectively, they said that sports stars and young people are "getting away" with self-promotion on social media channels in a way they wouldn't have before.

Until recently, Nishimura had only worked at traditional Japanese firms. Now she is with Ernst & Young and sees cultural differences regarding self-promotion expectations. Filling out her internal networking profile, including listing what she excelled at, was a first for her. She was told she needed to do it for any future promotions.

In traditional Japanese workplaces, the system of promotions is set. If you want a promotion, you don't communicate it. Takahashi, Hirose, and Gondo laughed when I asked how a person gets promoted. They said, "It's in the air." Gondo explained, "There isn't an English translation, but it's the concept of *sassuru*, which means to guess, presume, to read the other person," basically from thinking about them, knowing them, and observing their body language. "You don't say anything," Hirose said. "The other person just kind of reads your mind. That's the way you get promoted." People are expected to be mind readers.

## What Will People Say?

Many of us feel the effects of one of the most powerful four words spoken and unspoken: "What will people say?"

Piyali Mandal, a global strategic communications consultant who lives in Mumbai, says this question suppresses some people from doing what they really want because of the judgment, drama, and gossip associated with it. In an interview, she told me that the "What will people say?" rule of action "is an integral part of the culture and it starts with something as simple as you're raised in a family [where] you have to have long hair. 'What would others say if you cut your hair short?' What might seem like small things ends up applying to big things. There's a need for validation from others, to care what relatives, friends, and neighbors think. The 'people' can also be no one—an anonymous, faceless nobody. It's all about the people-pleasing that doesn't end. So even at work, you are there to please people and are too scared to ask [for] what you feel is rightfully yours."

Mandal points to Indra Nooyi, the former PepsiCo CEO and a hero for women, especially women in India. In an interview with *Fortune* magazine, Nooyi said of asking for a raise, "I find it cringeworthy. I cannot imagine working for somebody and saying my pay is not enough." She points to the cultural upbringing that taught her that if she did a good job, everything else would come with it. "It stopped me from asking for certain things," she said.

To that, Mandal said, "Imagine our personal first-rater feeling awkward about asking for something that she should have been asking for. That says a lot about where we stand as women leaders. So, I feel we really need to shed that inhibition about talking about our work."

In her consulting work, Mandal noted changes as Indians become global citizens within larger companies. "You are left with no other option but to speak for yourself," she said. "If you want to get a promotion, you must promote yourself first."

## "The Model Minority"

From a small town in China and now living in Ottawa, Canada's capital city, Jenny Chen has long carried a "work hard and succeed" pressure. Her highly successful career journey landed her the status of top financial advisor at a big bank, and now she's moved into a prominent corporate role. In an interview with me, she explained: "[There was the] combination of academic stereotypes, parental expectations, and minority status, so the bar was always really high for me and my siblings to succeed. However, I learned throughout my life that Asians, and even more so Asian women, were often told to shoot for the stars— but put your head down and don't ruffle feathers to get there. So, our experiences are shaped by stereotypes, including the model minority myth, characterizing us as polite rule-following groups who've achieved a higher level of success than the general immigrant population through some combination of innate talent and resilience."

It's a way that prioritizes hard work over speaking up to be recognized and promoted. The notion is that outworking everyone is the path to success, but it's the path to people-pleasing burnout.

"Unfortunately, these myths along with stereotypes in general erase the different experiences that impact each of us," Chen said. She purposefully shares her wins with her two young daughters but especially her failures to ensure they don't feel the pressure to perform and to live up to the stereotype.

## Sitting Eye to Eye

Brenda MacIntyre, or Medicine Song Woman, is a mixed-blood Cree woman and Sixties Scoop survivor. (The Sixties Scoop is a period in Canadian history, from the 1950s to the 1980s, during which government child welfare agencies forcibly removed many Indigenous children from their homes and communities. The children were raised in residential schools, foster care, or adopted into white families. The latter was MacIntyre's experience.) MacIntyre is a keynote speaker and an award-winning singer.

She told me, "When you sit with an Elder or Wisdom Keeper, you're going to get a lot of stories, but to ask them to write a bio about themselves—that's not going to happen. While storytelling is a natural gift we have always had, we live by example, walking our talk, so our actions and stories speak much more loudly than a bio can. We go through life with humility, always sitting eye to eye, each person equal in the circle. When everyone is eye to eye, heart to heart, building relationships and community, all life flourishes. Residential schools and intergenerational trauma destabilized healthy relationships and community, and stole our economy, so now we are reclaiming our Indigenous ways of knowing and being, and sharing our gifts widely with more success." For eons, we were all connected in a circle, linked and not ranked. This connected circle mindset is worth tapping into.

## The Tallest Poppy

Tall Poppy Syndrome occurs when people are criticized, alienated, disliked, or rejected because of their success and achievements. While my research noted that people in Canada, the UK, and New Zealand have experienced Tall Poppy Syndrome, people in Australia, the country that first labeled the syndrome, experience it most.

This phenomenon happens to people more frequently in their most intimate circles and social settings, including workplaces. There's a massive cost to the people it impacts and the organizations where this permeates. Those who are a cut above

● ● ●

# "Collaboration is the new competition."

**UNKNOWN**

the rest, high achievers, or different and eccentric will be cut down to meet the field of mediocre performers.

My friend Dr. Rumeet Billan, researcher and founder of Viewpoint Leadership, has studied and written about Tall Poppy Syndrome extensively. She noted, though, that you can flip the script. Think of the "cutter" as the one with the issue. Instead of internalizing the criticism, flip it back on them and realize they're likely going through something, so your success is a mirror back on them.

In a 2018 article, Dr. Billan wrote, "I recently heard someone say, 'Collaboration is the new competition.' If we can begin to let our guard down, begin to celebrate others instead of tearing them down, if we can work together instead of against each other, we can begin to shift the culture—to one where everything isn't a zero-sum game. If we learn that we are not lessened because someone else succeeds, we can start to open doors for others, and we can start to focus on developing self-worth, self-confidence and self-esteem."

## Who Toots Her Own Horn...

"Poser," "show-off," "know-it-all"—in the United Kingdom, there are plenty of informal and formal words for anyone who shines brighter than the next. This is about self-deprecation and being reserved. Several research respondents to the Bragging Rights survey said they know culturally not to "blow their own trumpet too loudly"; it's more about being "the master of the understatement."

As one research participant said of the British way to self-promote: "It's covert, doing it without seeming like you are doing it. Everyone is aware, but unless you get too excited about it, no one will call you on it." Another response was "Some people are very overt, others are very humble, the rest of us are trying to do it at a covert level." Another anonymous respondent wrote, "The English are big understaters. I am 'understating' in the understanding that people will know I'm understating and know I'm saying I've done very well indeed, actually." We'll unpack underbragging, humblebragging, and more in chapter 7.

## Competitive Bragging?

On the outside, the United States, with its highly individualistic society, seems to be the home of bragging and self-promotion. Look at American cowboys and politicians and rappers, who are legendary for their verbal artistry and a skill range that goes from making themselves sound conceited or dishonest to making themselves sound mythic. Often, these three groups land in the self-aggrandizement range with their put-downs of others. It's competitive bragging with even slight advantages tooted.

While I can point to these examples who (often) magnify things way out of proportion, so many in the population today downplay themselves, dim their light, and are conditioned socially to be humble too often.

And whether bragging is acceptable may depend on social status. As American author and small-business coach Jeffrey Shaw stated in his response to the Bragging Rights research survey, "Growing up in a lower socioeconomic group, to be conceited seemed like the worst thing. I'd say growing up in the lower-middle class was the biggest obstacle to overcome in becoming comfortable with self-promotion."

## Who Gets a Pass?

So who gets a pass on all these societal rules? Sports stars and coaches get a pass, as do movie stars and social media influencers. We celebrate these individuals as if doing so is a proxy for celebrating ourselves. Activists and writers are expected to draw attention to their work, and politicians and CEOs of large companies are also expected to talk about their performance, success, achievement, and wisdom all the time, in ways that are visible to select micro audiences they're specifically trying to influence, or to all of us.

Gender plays a huge factor in who gets a pass, as you've already seen in this book. I'm sure you have your own experiences and reflections. The gender spectrum is vast, and people from LGBTQ2S+ communities, whether they are out or not, may face large barriers at work, including microaggressions, discrimination, and isolation. In general, cis gender men tend to get a pass with bragging and self-promotion. Mary Ann Sieghart's book *The Authority Gap: Why Women Are Still Taken Less Seriously Than Men, and What We Can Do About It* is an excellent reference for an incisive intersectional analysis and deeper dive into the research.

People usually get a pass when someone invites them to a stage. Emelia Sam, a former associate professor of oral and maxillofacial surgery at Howard University, told me in an interview that she learned that lesson when she didn't have a carton of books to sell despite having just talked to a crowd of fifty people and mentioning her book, *I Haven't Found Myself, but I'm Still Looking*. Dr. Jeanne Sinkford, who was the first woman dean and first Black woman dean of an American dental school, had been on the stage earlier, and she turned to Sam and asked her where the book was. "And I just looked at her blankly," Sam said. "She's like, 'Look, if it were a man, he would have brought those books, and he would be promoting at this event right now, you know. So, next time you have something, you bring your book, but in the meantime, let me write a check. Just you remember you need to self-promote.' She bought books for everyone on the spot."

But practicing self-promotion has been hard for Sam. She said, "I spent the first few decades of my life dedicated to invisibility. There's a strange sort of push and pull between wanting to have a very visible platform, and then that thing that just makes you cringe and pull back."

Many of the people who get a pass are in highly visible roles. Visualizing career success in the knowledge economy is harder. When you're selling handcrafts, you can point to those beautiful items, but when you're consulting or working with data, your work is often less visible, which makes speaking up about it all the more valuable. In the next chapter, we'll look at some of the things that you can do to help yourself.

## ••• Bragging Right •••

A spiderweb of deeper structural issues, which my work here only hints at, keeps people from sharing their performance, success, and achievement with others.

**To Consider:** What cultural thinking influences your willingness to brag about yourself? In this sense, what works for you and what works against you?

**To Do:** Write a response to these questions:

- When do you wish you had been bolder?
- Reflect on a time when you were bold. What happened?

**To Share:** Which cultural norm on bragging reflects your experience? Talk about it with two work colleagues to hear their perspectives. The more we understand why we're wary of talking about success, the more we can change that.

# 5

# Programming Is Reality and Myth

As I write this, my twelve-year-old daughter, Elora, is singing her own power ballad. Here's what she's belting out as I type: "I'm unstoppable / you know / I'm invincible / Yeah, I don't want to live as an untold story / Oooh / Confidence is overrated / I'm so powerful / I don't need batteries, I say."

It's the ultimate empowerment song. The young have the right sense of empowerment. It might be because they're set in this world to consume, comment, and create. It seems that they've already nailed authenticity and vulnerability.

We spend a good deal of our time, especially after the age of twelve, fearing that we might be idiots and holding back from a host of ambitions. The truth is we're *all* absurd. We have no choice. Let that liberate you. It's our basic nature. You will be uncomfortable, and then you'll be comfortable (and the cycle will likely continue). It takes small steps of courage to get to confidence. Don't wait for more confidence. That's not what's holding you back.

But if a lack of confidence isn't holding you back, then what is? There are a few common denominators we'll explore in this chapter.

## You Belong in the Room

We often question whether or not we belong in the metaphorical room.

Vivian Pickard was a top executive at General Motors before leaving to run its foundation. Mentors of the highest esteem, such as Dr. Dorothy Height (who advised US presidents) and US civil rights activist Rosa Parks, cheered Pickard on early in her career. After forty years with GM, Pickard is retired but new, meaningful opportunities continue to come to her. In a podcast interview, she told me that when she started in the world of work, few women were in supervisory roles. When she began at a new level or was having a new experience, she'd talk to the other people with her to quickly realize, "I can do this. I don't think she's any smarter than I am." With each increasing level of responsibility, she'd say it over and over again to herself. She kept her mother's voice in her head: "You know what? You do belong. You can do this. You can do this. You do belong."

You belong in any room you want. Look to someone in your position or even a few steps ahead. What are they doing that you could easily start to do too?

## Under the Radar

Teri doesn't want a promotion, validation, or, frankly, to save the world. She's content where she is and does not want to chase the upward climb or add in any other opportunities. She's a widow and wants to put her energy into her children.

Staying where you are is a fine choice, but even to keep the status quo, you must be visible. We are continually being reassessed in a world of shifting priorities.

Unfortunately, Teri's boss is a tyrant, so her under-the-radar approach could never work. Professional invisibility is not a safe approach. If you've set up your job so you're in stealth mode, you're doing yourself a disservice. If you have a tyrant boss, work remotely, or are just one among many, people need to know you and the value you provide. This also applies to your clients; they need to know about your success and achievements. When people see you, it's harder for them to discount, ignore, or fire you. Dismissing people who hide is much less disruptive, so they're often the first to go.

You can increase your visibility simply by following up. During online meetings, send private direct messages after someone has made a good point. After discussions, send out a quick note of praise, especially to anyone outside your immediate team. It can be as simple as giving them kudos for their update. If your leader once removed is on a call, send a brief note of support for her point. To take it to the next level, you could also let them know that you're prepared to help them achieve their mission by action on XYZ items that align with your skills. These techniques work, even if you adopt them seemingly out of the blue. Make it a habit. Self-promotion is self-preservation. Ask yourself:

- Do people know what my contribution means to the company?
- What value do I bring every day or week?

It's great that you're rock solid and always deliver, but do they see that?

## The Imposter Experience

T.S. Eliot's question "If you aren't in over your head, how do you know how tall you are?" is the essence of imposter syndrome—I call it the *imposter experience*. We all experience it from time to time, when we are growing, leaping from understanding to experience to mastery. The path looks like an S-curve: when we begin, we think we know everything; then we realize we don't. It's that slow part where we feel overwhelmed and question ourselves. We're also likely impatient. Then we acquire more knowledge and skills, and our performance, success, and achievements increase. It's that sweet spot where you feel competence and confident. Then we get to mastery. Then we get bored and leap to another S-curve.

We count ourselves out of the running because of the constraints we put on ourselves and the real or perceived limitations others place on us. Here's an interesting fact: women usually wait until they have 100 percent of the qualifications listed for a job (which makes the move lateral), while some men will apply for a job on potential or as little as 60 percent of the listed criteria. Women's leadership expert Tara Sophia Mohr decided to research why and found that women hold back from applying because they want to follow the rules of the process. Women apply for fewer roles because they don't think they meet all the qualifications and thus would likely fail to be awarded the job. This goes back to our "being good girls" and following the rules. The reality is, though, others are taking the shot even though they don't have the qualifications. When I was actively hiring, I would include a note that said "If you have 70 percent of the qualifications and think you can do this job, then apply." We would get great candidates. You've got to reframe your beliefs so you can see yourself as being in a state of potential.

We are continually being reassessed in a world of shifting priorities.

So how to overcome the imposter experience? I acknowledge it when I feel it. "Hmm, isn't that interesting. I must be stretching." Be willing to admit you feel the experience, too, if someone shares their feelings with you. Let's normalize this as we all stretch out of our comfort zones. I always wonder, *Are we really growing if we don't feel it?* A powerful tool is taking ownership of our achievements rather than attributing our success to luck.

## Awkwardness and Shame

Most of us have a strong aversion to awkwardness—a form of embarrassment, discomfort, and sometimes shame.

That discomfort is often the result of a fixed mindset: we don't quite believe we can grow or that something doesn't have to be immediately perfect. We avoid the angst and discomfort and stay where we are. Instead, we need to adopt a growth mindset, which is a state of allowing ourselves to embrace the word "yet": "I'm not good at this—yet."

Shame runs along the same lines. Most of us don't try to do the biggest thing we're capable of because we're terrified of shame. Shame is an emotion conditioned into so many of us as children. It is packed into our cultures through beliefs, behaviors, worldviews, and stories. Shame is often ingrained in school and places of worship. Our parents, who got it from their parents, reinforced it in us.

Of course, we do need some shame. It keeps us from acting out of pure self-interest. But it can also be a tool others use over us. Those with higher levels of shame-proneness and self-criticism stay with shame longer than needed. Shame makes us look even further inward and spreads a negative light on our entire self-view. We spiral into it. It's an emotion created in our brains, but it's a hard one to control.

Victoria was feeling shame days after a big speech. She thought she could wing it and didn't practice enough, and it didn't go well. She told herself that she was so ashamed, that she was a big failure and would never recover from the botched speech. I coached her to reframe the feelings as guilt: "I feel guilty that I didn't practice enough to deliver to the level of expectation I had in my mind." Then she committed to practicing in advance with a coach to ensure her next time was better (and it was). The commitment was the responsible action. She was going to do something to atone for her mistake. Not practicing was a mistake instead of an inward reflection of Victoria. It's not how she always is; she just messed up this speech.

Shame resilience is a true challenge. I'm continually reminding myself that to be seen and heard, and put yourself out into the world in a meaningful way, you have to embrace the notion that shame is part of the journey.

Sometimes we have to step into being uncomfortable to grow, and that's true for being seen and heard. It's a new muscle that needs to be worked and stretched. If (and when) you mess up bragging, or any of your self-promotion tactics, know that resilience is key. Dust yourself off and get back to it.

## Fear of Being Seen

"Today's news is tomorrow's chip wrapper." That's a quote from Mark Bowden's mentor. Bowden is a body language keynote speaker, author, and communication coach. When we talked, he explained, "It's an English idea that whatever is on the front page of a newspaper today, tomorrow they'll be eating chips off

"Love yourself first and everything else falls into line. You really have to love yourself to get anything done in this world."

LUCILLE BALL

of it." (The Brits used to wrap everything, including french fries, in old newspapers.)

Bowden makes as many videos as he can to help his clients and those who follow his expertise, knowing that the posts will potentially be well down the social media feed the next day. In our chat, he mentioned Canadian CEO and celebrity Arlene Dickinson. She was on the cover of an obscure magazine, then on social media, and then on reality TV (*Dragons' Den*, the equivalent to *Shark Tank*). It didn't matter that the first few magazine covers Dickinson appeared on were disposable. Dickinson is visible all the time. She's everywhere. Bowden said, "Day after day after day, the trust built, so she became front of mind... Now she's one of the most recognizable women in Canada."

Bowden said the only time you should worry about being seen is if what you're doing "is illegal or offensive; if it's either, then maybe think about it again. Otherwise, put it out there. Also, do you care who you're offending? They may not be your audience. Who cares? It's got to be legal. Otherwise, it's never going to be so bad that you shouldn't put yourself out there."

It takes grit to show up day after day and put yourself out there sharing your ideas, vision, and successes.

## Envy and Admiration

We often hold back from bragging because we don't want to make other people feel bad or jealous, but, in fact, we don't know what will trigger someone to be envious or admire us. In my coaching, and in the Bragging Rights research, I've found that some people point to their family as the reason they limit their self-promotion; their family members don't accept or acknowledge their successes. It's difficult to deal with a lack of understanding and support. Your family may be used to seeing you only one way, so there's comparison and resistance. While we are responsible for what we share, others are responsible for how they receive our messages. We can remember that as we practice bragging.

On a recent video call, my daughter and her friends talked as they walked around their bedrooms. They all had awards hanging on the walls, and the girls listened to each other and asked questions about the awards and how they had won them. *What a strong, healthy perspective,* I thought. It was an entirely envy-free exchange of bragging. They all had different successes they could share. We are always modeling to our children, and clients give this as a reason they want to self-promote: they want their children to see their professional successes so they can "see it to be it."

When you see a post or hear someone who inspires envy in you, ask them to tell you more. Ask them how they got there. What was a pivotal moment? Compare yourself only to who you were yesterday—it's the only competitor on the same field.

## Narcissism

Many avoid bragging because they worry about being seen as a narcissist, but bragging, for reasons I've established so far in this book, is essential to positive self-esteem. A Research Brief article that looked at 437 studies on narcissism defined the personality style as "entitled self-importance." Narcissism exists on a spectrum. At one extreme, you have someone who tends to be disrespectful, with an exaggerated sense of self-importance and overinflated confidence. At the other end is the insecure and arrogant individual who needs and wants external validation. You might dip into any part of the continuum, but it's only an issue if it is a pattern of behavior. Everyone has some degree of narcissism. With normal narcissism, a healthy dose of self-esteem helps a person thrive. Researchers have found what you might already suspect—that narcissism is on the rise, but they've also found that it might actually be healthy for the broader cultural change going on because of technology: "Narcissism may be a functional and healthy strategy for dealing with the modern world."

## For All Personality Types

Bragging and self-promotion are challenging for most, but it can be even harder for shy people. As Susan Cain, author of *Quiet: The Power of Introverts in a World That Can't Stop Talking*, explains, "Shyness is about the fear of social judgment."

Many of the suggestions in Part 2 of this book can help, as can focusing on talking about your work and how it matters, removing the "self" from your mind as you self-promote.

Introverts might also put their hands up in protest because bragging looks like an extrovert's game. Introverts get their energy from being in their own company and having time to recharge alone. They may appear reserved, but that's not always the case. They often process things internally. An extrovert derives energy from other people. They might be very talkative and often process thoughts out loud to others, but not always.

A less familiar term is "ambivert." It's the balance of both introvert and extrovert—ambiverts enjoy others but need their time alone—and most of us are actually that. We can flip into either realm depending on the context, goals, or mood. I'm an ambivert. I'll have a great time giving a speech or workshop, and enjoy lunch or dinner with you, but I like to head to my room and regain my energy. I need time to recharge, but I happily adapt and adjust.

Any personality type can do self-promotion—including introverts. It needn't be grandstanding, smarmy work. It shouldn't be. You can do this in a secure, balanced, and assured way, using the tactics and tools that suit you.

## ••• Bragging Right •••

Brag to yourself first. Believe in your performance, experience, and wisdom. That will help you overcome the norms, myths, stereotypes, and expectations around bragging. It will help you be your own advocate first.

**To Consider:** What's your personal anthem? If you were to walk on stage right now, what song would you want them to play to introduce you? Why that song? My anthem would be "Could Have Been Me" by The Struts. The song is about seizing the day with no regret, not listening to the trolls or my inner critic, and knowing that while some days my plans won't work out, I need to keep going. As a bonus, it reminds me to channel my inner rock star.

**To Do:** Think about the wins from the past five years. Take a minute to think about each year. These don't have to be masterpieces or life-altering wins; they can be anything you thought was a win, small and large. Jot them down.

Now pick one win. Set a timer for three minutes. Write down, in point form, ten great things you can say about your win.

**To Share (a):** Do the exercise above with a partner, exchanging wins so you can talk each other up too.

**To Share (b):** Ellen Johnson Sirleaf, former president of Liberia, said: "If your dreams do not scare you, they're not big enough. The size of your dreams must always exceed your current capacity to achieve them... If you start off with a small dream, you may not have much left when it is fulfilled because, along the way, life will... make demands on you."

# 6

# The Need to Partner

MANY OF us believe that trees compete for sunlight, with the winners shading out the losers—survival of the fittest. In reality, underground, trees are helping, guiding, and nurturing each other and the greater ecosystem. This is what Sara Curleigh-Parsons, Deborah Aarts, and I were considering while helping a Fortune 300 company with storytelling and employee engagement. Several key units needed to move from service-based thinking to thinking about how they transform lives. If they didn't, they'd be competing against technology the company had developed for clients with simpler needs. We hoped that refocused teams would help clients with more complex matters, or those who wanted the expert-level advice to transform their lives. If these units moved upmarket, they'd be partners in the success of the company.

As business leaders with different areas of expertise, Sara, Deborah, and I have an alliance. When we collaborate, we have intention and purpose, but we're on the lookout for how we can help each other, guide, and give each other business. We could have easily staked our ground as competitors.

Deborah and I became friends when she was employed with a national magazine that hosted the fastest-growing company awards and events. We met in 2017 when my company ranked in the top 100, and when my company ranked again the following year, she put me on a panel and included me in blurbs throughout the magazine. We kept in touch infrequently, through social platforms, and when I had job postings she reached out with recommendations of some awesome people in her network. Those people now work regularly with me. Several years later, Deborah decided to go freelance. That's when I knew there would be opportunities for us to partner.

It was literally a lightning strike that brought Sara and me together. We met during a torrential downpour and lightning storm that stranded us on an island in beautiful Stony Lake, Ontario. She's a Canadian expat who has been living in the UK for more than thirty years and was on the lake for a visit. We shared what was going great with our businesses. We quickly figured out our strengths (with no self-deprecating). There are overlaps in our businesses: we're both facilitators helping companies with stakeholder engagement through workshops, and we're both passionate about empowering storytelling.

When Sara went back to the UK, I followed up from time to time to keep in touch. She came back another summer and we decided to take our sharing deeper to talk about our pricing, methods, approaches, and frameworks. It helped both of our businesses. By talking easily about our offers and value, we were able to grow a connection and bond. We put it out there by seeing each other.

Then the power of partnerships really kicked in. We got to work together. I asked Sara and Deborah to cocreate a project with me. Sara then brought me in to help her with a UK firm expanding into North America. She also introduced me to a wider network, where more opportunities have landed. We bring each other in front of different audiences we wouldn't have had on our own. On the outside, we three would be seen as competitors, but on the inside, we're making huge magic together as collaborators.

It might seem that bragging is an individualistic pursuit, but the heart of this book is about how you can show up for others and make a ruckus. Interconnectedness, working in harmony, and drawing out each other's strengths and then learning from the overlaps are huge. To go further, farther, faster, we need to go together. We must relinquish the myth of the lone creator.

Jacqueline Novogratz is an entrepreneur and author. In her book *Manifesto for a Moral Revolution*, she revises the Golden Rule—treat others as you want to be treated—instead making it: "Give more to the world than what you take from it." It is a moral reimagining, an invitation to think about what we're giving instead of what we're extracting. This is about service. Instead of thinking the world owes us something, we consider what we might offer. Entitlement is the downfall of bragging. If we feel and act entitled, others are turned off.

Bragging is also about attracting others who want to do the work we want to do in the world. We need the courage to tell our truths, put the signal out to each other, ask for help, then lift each other. In a conversation with Hatch Network, Novogratz said, "Identity can and should also be used as a tool to connect us. All of us have within us multiple identities, and when one is threatened, too often, that's all we become and that's all we let somebody else be."

Those around us can propel us beyond someone of identical skill—connections make the difference. We are community-made, not self-made and the data proves it. Albert-László Barabási, whom I mentioned earlier, has been studying the "math behind our social fabric" as part of his "universal laws of success." His definition of success is specific: it is "the rewards we earn from the communities we belong to." This is distinct from our performance. We do have to perform, and we must be good, but when performance can't be measured, networks drive success. Barabási said of his research:

> Performance is what you do: how fast you run, what kind of paintings you paint, what kind of papers you publish. However, in our working definition, success is about what the community notices from what you did, from your performance: How does it acknowledge it, and how does it reward you for it? In other terms, your performance is about you, but your success is about all of us. And this was a very important shift for us, because the moment we defined success as being a collective measure that the community provides to us, it became measurable, because if it's in the community, there are multiple data points about that.

Barabási can measure and mark success paths, but what *we* can take away is that you must master networking—connecting and building relationships with others to truly succeed.

In construction, they use the term "sistering" to describe adding a second support to strengthen an area that isn't quite strong enough, such as floor joists. Jacki Zehner, an investor and former partner at Goldman Sachs, has developed a mantra based on this term: "We are sistering up in acknowledgment that there are still huge inequities and power structures that exist, and which result in gender-related disparities. By sistering up, we will accelerate positive change."

I used to use "wingman" to mean the person we connect with for support and to do good things, but I never thought it quite fit. "Sistering up" is more accurate, as it supports all involved. This is sharing our hopes, dreams, and challenges with each other. Then we ask and consider what we can do to help others, and we ask for support too. Building these professional bridges can

When we join with others, our individual and collective stories become amplified and stronger.

span organizational boundaries, so think outside of your office, company, industry, and background.

Another way to look at this is through the lens of "shine theory." Coined by writer Ann Friedman and her podcast co-host, digital strategist Aminatou Sow, shine theory states that if women collaborate with each other rather than competing, it boosts everyone's success. We all shine. It redresses the cliché that in relationships, professional or otherwise, women are jealous of each other.

We encourage empathy for those who struggle and grieve over losses, but we also need to coax our minds to celebrate when people soar. Empathy means considering and sensing what other people are feeling not only when they're hurting but also when they're happy. Researchers have given this conscious sharing in others' joyful experiences a name: *freudenfreude*. Similar to what Buddhists call *mudita*, or when English-speaking Yiddish dabblers use the word "kvell," *freudenfreude* is "the lovely enjoyment of another person's success" even when it doesn't directly involve us. It's the opposite of schadenfreude, the shameful joy or self-satisfaction one feels at someone else's losses, pain, or misfortune. Schadenfreude has gotten much airtime in popular culture.

In a paper in the *World Journal Psychiatry and Mental Health Research*, psychologist Catherine Chambliss found that the lack of an empathetic response from those we share our success with can cause relationship failure (her primary investigation was on depression). The takeaway is: don't blow out someone else's flame.

In her book *Atlas of the Heart*, Brené Brown has this tip when talking about your success: "When someone demonstrates joy when we share ours, we can express gratitude: 'Thank you for celebrating this with me. It means so much that you're happy for me.'" See more on *freudenfreude* and your teams in chapter 13.

Look for times to collaboratively brag. These are opportunities to give genuine compliments, share credit with others, and let someone be in the spotlight with you. I know many people are concerned that when they claim credit or talk about themselves, they won't appear very likeable, which is why we tend toward self-deprecation, thinking it will make us more socially acceptable (but that often backfires). When you're in a community with other successful people, talking about your success is often the norm, and you'll find that others want to help you be even more successful. Let me explain with this example: Dr. Andrea Wojnicki and I have similar clients, and some of our clients have overlapped. You might think we're competitors, but we're not. We're collaborators. She just had me on her podcast, *Talk About Talk*. It was so much fun. We gave each other nuggets of wisdom and language we didn't have before that will help our clients, and we also lifted each other up. By both of us shining, we brought more light to our work. We're sending several social signals, too, that I want to point out. By showcasing our individual knowledge of our material, we're signaling that we're competent; by sharing the spotlight with someone else (and helping each other shine), we're demonstrating confidence and that we're experts, willing to take a risk. It's a win-win to share the spotlight.

## Radical Generosity

Vicki Saunders, the founder of Coralus, a community of radical generosity with members who are committed to transforming themselves and global systems by collectively working on the

"The success of every woman should be the inspiration to another. We should raise each other up."

SERENA WILLIAMS

world's to-do list, never put her hand up as a kid. In an interview, she told me that as an adult, she never went to the microphone—until the day she did. Sitting in front of her was an audience of 1,500 people waiting for her to speak. She said that, with legs shaking the whole time behind the lectern, she was "bad, really bad." Now, she's in front of thousands of people all the time. "I don't need to hide anymore, but it's been a real journey. I think this is why I have the empathy that I have for people. I can feel the pain of everybody as they're going through things. I can see it. I know how hard it is."

Of the Coralus community, Saunders said, "You don't just say 'Suck it up. Just take the mic, go do it.' But you come back to that time and remember what it was like when you were shaking and how hard it was. It's important to give people space to acknowledge that and let them know they're not going to die if they do this. It's going to be okay. You can get through it. One of the greatest gifts we can give each other is 'I see you, and jump off the cliff. You're stronger than you think you are.'" Community gives you resilience and a jumping-off point for action. When we put off doing something, Saunders said, "It gets bigger and bigger until you deal with it. The sooner you kind of get thrown off the cliff to try these things, the better, because then your story about it doesn't get so gargantuan. Most of us make this stuff up and make it seem so hard. It's just getting to do it that's hard."

Much of this comes down to mindset and believing that there is enough to go around, rather than hoarding or operating from fear. When times get tough, we need a generosity of spirit.

There is a concern that as you become visible, especially as a woman, the critics show up. Often right after a victory, a backlash occurs. You can flip the script, however, and not fear haters but take them as a measure of success when they show up.

You know your work is getting in front of many people when the trolls show up. Ann Friedman wrote, "Haters aren't something to be feared... They're validation that you're a big deal. And they're fuel to do better. Now you're inspired to prove that their jealousy is warranted."

I'm sure the criticism won't make you feel great when it happens. But if you build up your network of allies, when the bullies come for you, a strong contingent will defend you so that you can continue doing your good. Take in any just criticism, but only from people you respect and who respect you.

### ••• Bragging Right •••

When we join with others, our individual and collective stories become amplified and stronger. If they know what you stand for, what you're capable of, and what success you've had, like-minded people will see how your work fits in with theirs—and vice versa—and everyone will benefit. You'll have leverage. You'll have the power to help those who are invisible be seen and heard. You'll create exponential impact.

**To Consider:** It is okay to be friends with a competitor. Look at a person a bit ahead of you and where you are. Ask yourself, "Would we be better as collaborators than as competitors?" The answer is almost always yes.

**To Do:** Shine the light on others. Find someone who you know has been underappreciated and give her laurels. Tell her why she matters to you. Lifting others up and shining a light on them amplifies you, too, in more ways than you'll ever realize.

Use this quote from American social-political activist Gloria Steinem to inspire you: "I understand that I'm supposed to be passing the torch to you. So, I just want to tell you I'm not, because the image of having only one torch is part of the problem[,] not the solution. I'm keeping my torch, and I'm helping to light other people's torches. Only when each of us [has] our own full, unique blazing torch will we be able to light our path to the future."

**To Share:** Set up a "Bragging Rights" session. Pick some awesome people whom you trust and practice sharing your accomplishments and successes together without hesitation or limitations. Take turns, ideally going around in a circle.

To enhance the experience, select as diverse a group as possible in terms of experiences, industry, and background. Let others catch you if you become self-deprecating and do the same for them. Trust yourselves to brag. You're already in a group of admirers.

Use the following prompts, with everyone taking time to reflect before answering:

- "The best thing about me is..."
- "I am grateful for..."
- "I desire..."

After one member answers these three phrases aloud, the group should say in unison: "And so it shall be, or something better." Repeat this exercise with each person, until you've all had a turn answering the three questions and everyone has received the group affirmation.

# PART TWO
# HOW TO OWN YOUR BRAGGING RIGHTS

**IT IS TIME TO DELVE** into how to be seen and heard. I've thought about the saying "It's not what you know, it's who you know" at various times in my life, then extended it to "who knows you," but once I started to break this down, I realized that this adage is not going to last. Competence is clearly essential, now and as the world becomes even more competitive. I developed seven points to make a Bragging Rights Strategy that you can use to develop your personalized plan for bragging and purposeful self-promotion.

It works for everyone, from CEOs with forty years of experience who are used to being in the spotlight as part of their job to those just starting in the professional world.

## Bragging Rights Strategy

How are you?
Who are you?
Who do you serve?
What do you know?
Who do you know?
Who knows you?
What's next?

**How are you?** What mindset affects your bragging and self-promotion? Imposter experience, Tallest Poppy, something else? Having a growth mindset will help you. Know that emotional discomfort is part of a growth mindset. Mindset is foundational, so it is integrated throughout this book.

**Who are you?** What are your perspectives and passions, and what is your brand promise?

**Who do you serve?** Who makes up your minimum viable audience? You don't need to talk to everyone, but you need to talk to *someone*. Your audience can be of one or a hundred—just know whom you are meant to help and talk to them.

**What do you know?** What do you love to talk about? You can be generous with your knowledge, and you don't need to know everything. You can also grow on a promise of knowing. An "I have a certificate" form of knowing is not required.

**Who do you know?** Who would love to help you? You likely already have many people around you, so tap into those who already care, knowing you can also help them. Network with strategy.

**Who knows you?** What do the people who know you say about you? You've done the work to draw attention to you. People understand what you do, whom you do it for, and how you can help others. You have social currency and you're set up to attract people to you.

**What's next?** How can people help you get where you are going faster? You want people to know what's next for you so they align with your goals.

These seven points are interconnected and woven throughout Part 2. On LisaBragg.com, I share some models to help you further visualize this work.

Even if you have done professional branding exercises with your public relations and communications team, go through Part 2 carefully as an individual. We're so often asked to think about our role within a company, but this exercise is about *you* in your professional journey. Your positional influence will change over time. Going through and applying the lessons ahead will help you become even more valuable in your current role and help your future self be ready no matter where your path takes you.

# 7

# How to Self-Promote

THIRTY MINUTES after author Michael Bungay Stanier sent the first draft of his next book to his editor, he posted a picture to a social media account. That simple post gave a kick to my brain and that creeping feeling of being a fraud swept over me. I should have posted a similar picture because I, too, had just hit send to my editor. Instead, the photo I took to remember the moment was safely tucked away on my phone. That photo of me with tired eyes and hair swept up into a messy half-ponytail wasn't going to be posted in public. I was going to take a better one the next day, after I had slept, put some makeup on, and looked coiffed.

Not posting that messy-haired, dark-circled-eyed photo goes against what I tell you to do in this book and what I will show you how to do in this chapter. Until I saw Michael's photo, I wasn't reflecting on the importance of the moment. He was planting the seeds of his future. He was sharing this moment, this glimpse of success, not just for himself but for those who follow and engage with him. I stopped hiding and posted the picture that showed the late nights and early mornings, no makeup, the tea-ringed desk, the reality. And yes, people showed up for me on my post as they did for Michael, excited to know that I had something of value to share with them.

Bragging is talking about yourself with pride. As I've said, this includes your successes, performances, achievements, skills, experiences, and wisdom. We often wait for a result or culminating activity, that major milestone to share, but skilled braggers bring people along on the journey. They build rapport. Your audience wants to see the moments and the milestones, but the magic of moments counts for much more. By seeing your moments, we also believe in your significant milestones more, you build up more social currency in our minds, and we want to celebrate with you. Often, those you've brought on the journey are also more invested in your success.

You might be setting yourself up for the next stage, knowing that your time as CEO of your firm is coming to an end in two to three years. Time to start positioning for boards (and wouldn't it be nice to be in the hall of fame for your industry as you leave it?). You might already have the spotlight, by doing speeches and representing your company, but now it's time to harness that power to make it work for you. Bragging and self-promotion are business skills that aren't taught to most of us. You might be looking to use it to move from overworked to competitive without having to go to every networking event (who has time or energy?) because you're on the lookout for your next role (and maybe you're not quite trusting the path that seemed set for you five years ago).

Your mission for self-promotion will be unique to you. I do it to get my ideas out into the world (and to test them), to get on new stages, and to gain new opportunities and new partners for collaborations. Some of my clients have done it because they are bored with their current roles and see it as a springboard to being relevant and for their future pivot. Others use it to recruit new clients. In some work environments, self-promotion is the only way to get a new role or a raise. Every single one of us needs to self-promote to future-proof our professional journey.

Self-promotion carries your bragging further out into the world, through amplification mechanisms such as posting on social media, making videos, applying for awards, joining networks, writing articles, and sending emails. The reality is self-promotion is often reactive. People get into a flurry of self-promotion when they need to pivot, or reinvent, which are okay times to start. Still, by regularly engaging in self-promotion no matter the conditions, you'll win more opportunities frequently, and you will be creating the safety net you need. There is no single ultimate destination. You will take these steps of success over and over again. It's an achievement orientation to be responsible for your successes (and failures). Think of having your own generator set up for when and if your current situation dims. Those small beacons of self-promotion about your performance along the way are opportunities to show others your abilities. If you let your achievements go unnoticed, proving that your performance is tied to ability after the fact is more difficult.

You're not alone in wanting to do more. The data from the Bragging Rights research shows that 85 percent said, "I need to self-promote more." And 90 percent agreed that they need to self-promote to further their careers.

Wherever you are—pivoting, reinventing, reacting, or looking to add more to your tool kit—you need to start bragging and self-promoting today so you'll be ready for the future you want. It is a long-term process that needs consistency. Start to find the energy to do this work so you'll include it as part of your schedule. It should account for 20 percent of your work time (it's valuable to your work), but that's not likely realistic as you start to integrate it into your life. I'm not going to push you into full-time content creator mode, either, where you're developing videos and podcasts and writing posts all day. Do what you can, but know that content creation is only one facet. Any time you allocate for content, know that most of it should be to amplify what you've already produced.

I'm going to give you some self-promotion tips right now and some pitfalls to avoid before we get into personalizing your path in the next chapter.

## Self-Promotion Primer

Self-promotion starts by walking in the door. Come in as a ten. We often hide or diminish ourselves so that we reveal our strengths over time, or we position a peg or two lower thinking we'll slowly work up to showing our awesomeness. Instead, be intriguing from the outset. Walking in as your highest self is the secret to success, according to Vivian Pickard, whom you met in chapter 5. She told me, "Don't diminish yourself," especially at the beginning. "You have to show up as a ten," she said. "If I show up as a three, if my package is a three, then I am going to have to work to build up to that eight, nine, or ten." If you show up as less than you are, you won't likely move up very far. First impressions count. Don't diminish yourself from the start.

### Go First

In TV news, I always wanted to be the first one to ask a question. Reporters know that any minute, the interview subject might walk away. The person who goes first also sets the tone and frequently receives more consideration of their question in business too. I often like to go first. As I told my daughter before going ziplining for the first time, this is partly so that I don't have to watch other people get freaked out—that scares me more.

Don't wait to hear everyone else speak first. If you have an idea, contribute it, however big or small. People are more likely to remember you, which gives you social currency. Remember my TED Talk? I went first (I didn't have a choice), and many people remembered me because of it: "Oh, yes, you were first and you talked about..."

Show up early to everything, as well. For an online meeting, the moderator and expert might have opened the room. At an in-person event, at the beginning it's quiet and you can figure out the lay of the land. It's easier to meet people who will stick with you. It also allows you to leave early if you need to and still be remembered.

**Don't Bury the Lede**

We add so many qualifiers to our communication, especially social media posts, that we divert people's attention away from the very information we want them to receive. In journalism, this is called "burying the lede," which means hiding your point below other information that isn't as critical to know. We do it because we've been taught to dim our light and to be socially humble. You might also be doing it because of so many examples of people diminishing themselves (so, doing it wrong) on social media.

Get to the point quickly without qualifiers and platitudes. Let's say you want people to know that you won an award for being awesome, but you start by talking about how you are humble, then you thank a long list of people, then talk about someone who inspires you, and then finally you get to the award. Phew. Feels like an Oscar speech when the actor doesn't respect the clock.

Keep it tight and be authentic. People ask me all the time about how to write about winning an award. My friend Dr. Cranla Warren says you have to "own it, and articulate it, without apology." She's a researcher on arrogance (so she should know, right?) and the vice president of leadership development at the Institute for Health and Human Potential. Here's her post about an award she won:

> What a weekend!
>
> So very proud to have been recognized and celebrated as one of 2022's 100 Accomplished Black Canadian Women at the formal gala held in Toronto, Canada. Thank you so very much for this honor 100 Accomplished Black Canadian Women Project. So much energy, courage, and care in one room—you are making a difference!

Dr. Niro Sivanathan, a professor at London Business School, has researched influence extensively. He says we think that our thoughts add up, but "in the mind of the receiver, they average out." His research also gives us this gem: quality trumps quantity. "By increasing the number of arguments, you do not strengthen your case, but rather you actively weaken it." My point here is that listing off your credibility is another way to bury the lede.

Nicola, an executive in supply chain management, spent a large portion of time opening a speech she was giving by wrapping her credentials around her like a security blanket. Despite advice from other speakers to drop the lengthy intro, she took five minutes and forty-three seconds to essentially read off her CV. Then she got into the reason she was talking to the room of stakeholders. Nicola said, "I want them to know that I'm credible, and all of those points make it real."

Unfortunately, the opposite happened. Nicola had credibility as soon as she appeared in the rundown of the event, because the audience trusted the organizers to schedule someone worthy of their time and attention. But her lengthy justification made them start to question her credibility.

Showing up is self-promotion. You have to be in the way to get your way.

Having a robust online presence makes it easy for people to search you if they want to know about your credentials. It's there that you can talk in depth about what makes you worthy of your position.

**Get On Social Media**
The platform you like most is the best platform. Commenting on others' posts is the easiest way to be seen, but to have a greater impact, you need to post your thoughts. Posting with consistency will gain you traction.

Use social media to reach out to people who will be at a conference you're attending. It helps to have friends in advance. Once you've met them, take a picture with them and share it. I do this all the time and have more relationships that last that way. We're excited to meet each other, and then we have a way of continually following up. I also regularly connect with the experts who will be there, and it has helped get me one-on-one time with them. They might have extra time for a coffee before heading back to the airport, as I often do. If not, they're at least aware of you. You can apply this to any stakeholders you want to connect with on a deeper level. The point is that they'll feel like they already know you. You're a slightly familiar face in a sea of people. (I often get hugs after just one contact.)

**Take Pictures**
Remember Michael Bungay Stanier's post I mentioned earlier? Taking pictures that represent your wins and posting them is a simple way to reach people. For example, Fatima received a gift from the C-suite for whom she'd provided a service. She took a picture of it and included it in her thank-you email and sent it to her leader. That leader then sent it up to a range of leaders. It spread. Not only did Fatima look good, but her leader did,

too, for sharing her win widely. Her win was his win. It helped give him a better profile, too, with more proof points of his great team.

## Access the Hidden Powerhouse

I always recommend finding out who the true influencers are in any organization. This could be the one you directly work for or the one you are consulting with. Influencers could be external consultants or former employees, and don't ever forget assistants. Assistants are *the* strategic influencers. Get to know these people as soon as you can, and be generous. Informal opinion leaders can be the most unassuming, least "powerful" people in the room and yet they have the ear of everyone.

If you've read any detective stories such as those with Sherlock Holmes, you know that what's on the surface isn't the only story. The storyline often serves multiple agendas. Business has that mystery too. You need to do some sleuthing to know what's really going on behind the scenes. Who wants what and why (at the human-to-human level)? You'll find that you'll get more opportunities and credit much easier if you can connect the dots. In an article for *Harvard Business Review*, author and researcher Liz Wiseman noted that "you can ascertain what's important by paying attention to what your leaders are spending their time on, what is being talked about, what has momentum, and what is celebrated. *That's* the agenda. Find the connection between your stakeholder's agenda and the work you are doing right now. Let them know that you are the *how* to their *what*. Try crafting a short statement that captures how your work will help them achieve the priorities on their agenda. If you send a periodic status report, consider revamping it to communicate two critical points: 1) What you understand to be the most important work and 2) How you are working on what's most important. You're sure to get a different reaction." I'll add—send that status report. It's social currency.

Wiseman continued: "If you want your work to land with impact, worry less about whether people 'get you' and worry more about whether your leaders and stakeholders know you understand what's important—that you 'get it.'" Once they know you get it, it is so much easier for them to "get you." Mystery solved.

### Take On an Official Capacity

Have some time to put on an event? Many experts host mastermind dinners with people they admire. You might host a small group coffee and chat. People are thrilled to be included, and it helps your social standing as a connector. This is a great tip for people who are shy because you can research the people and curate to whom you want to extend yourself. It makes networking easier, as it can give you confident energy.

## Social Media (Personal and Professional)

People sometimes ask me whether they should have two accounts for social media, one personal and one professional. The answer is different for everyone. Just know that, even if you have different accounts, whatever you post anywhere can show up everywhere. So you need to post with intention.

People from your professional life will want to follow you on all your channels, and the same goes for friends and family. The lines are fuzzy, especially as clients become friends and friends become clients in a peer-to-peer economy.

The blurry time we live in can be especially tricky if you're trying to be an influencer with a "personal brand" that doesn't align with your professional life. For example, during the pandemic, at a time when Canada was advising against nonessential travel, a manager of the government agency urging people not to travel took a controversial trip under her personal brand as a fashion and travel influencer. She apologized for it, but then a short time later quit the government to follow her dreams of becoming a full-time social media influencer.

## Wallflowers Beware

Showing up is self-promotion. You have to be in the way to get your way. The more exposure you have to more people, the more likely you'll get the opportunities you want.

In some cases, this means literally standing up. Waiting around when people are gathering can be awkward, but if you do so standing up, people are more likely to approach you. It shows you are open. Sitting looking at your phone signals that you are closed.

Where you sit in an office or coworking space matters too. Sit near the formal or informal decision makers or the people you want to influence. Proximity bias is real, so when you are present, make sure people see you. If you're online only, be sure to show up early and be ready if there's a chance to catch up with someone during a break. There is nothing wrong with doing a second five-minute video call when there's a break. If you are on camera and presenting, standing gives you more energy and focuses the attention on you.

● ● ●

"I've learned what's the better win: me sitting at a table or us sitting at a table? Don't be convinced to fight for one spot. Instead fight for multiple spots."

LILLY SINGH

## Scripts for Sharing Your Wins

In the 1970s, beauty brand L'Oréal needed to convince women to buy its hair color over competing products, though it was more expensive. Ilon Specht was a twenty-three-year-old copywriter working at McCann Erikson, an ad agency, when she wrote the revolutionary copy for L'Oréal's hair color campaign. The premise was that the woman featured in the advertisements didn't mind paying more for L'Oréal *because*, she said of herself, *"I'm* worth it." As Malcolm Gladwell stated in an article for the *New Yorker* in 1999, this campaign stood out because the "model herself spoke, directly and personally." Usually, these types of advertisements were "other-directed," meaning that it was others commenting on the model's looks. But in L'Oréal's hair color commercial, actor Joanne Dusseau took up the full frame, walked forward while the camera tracked back, and talked about herself without apology. It was such a hit that L'Oréal's slogan became "Because I'm worth it." It now alternates between "because you're worth it" and "because we're worth it" as well.

The word "because" is a powerful tool when bragging. It can connect even a subjective statement to objective proof. For example, "I landed this big client *because* I paid close attention to the organization's needs and provided an example of our exemplary processes before they signed on."

Because you're worth it: if you are having trouble putting words to the good work you do, here are some starter statements to try (these work like magic):

**"Here's my contribution..."** This statement works in multiple contexts, including those where bragging is not highly regarded and when pointing out your contributions to a team project. If someone claims your work, you might also use statements such as "I appreciate [name] adding to my thinking" or "I'm glad we're on the same page. My original thinking is that…"

**"People tell me that…"** This softens a brag, as you've put it in the third person.

**"I'm proud to have supported my client by…"** This is a softer version of "I did this…"

**"It's a privilege to have…"** Other variations of this include "I was excited when…," "I was honored by…," and "I appreciate…"

Banish the statements "It was really a team effort" and "It wasn't a big deal" from your vocabulary. It's also stronger to talk about accomplishments rather than effort.

I asked Whitney Johnson, who is recognized as one of the world's foremost executive coaches, what she recommends her clients say when they're having trouble bragging. One suggestion of particular note is:

> I know it might feel odd for me to talk to you about what I do well because society has taught us to not like women who do. But now I'm going to, so that you will know that I can do the work you are thinking of hiring me to do.

Andrea Wojnicki, whom you might remember as founder of *Talk About Talk*, has a great gem to soften a brag, which she uses when she's concerned the audience might perceive a brag as showing off. Talking to me, she explained, "I was a student at Harvard Business School. While it's a fantastic institution, I know that sometimes people think Harvard alumni brag. Some Harvard alumni do brag; we have a name for that. We call it the 'H-bomb.' So does that mean that I should avoid telling people that I went to Harvard? Well, I also know that when companies are considering hiring me, my Harvard education can establish credibility."

So, here's her strategy to deal with it: "I tell people when I'm introducing myself that I earned my doctorate at Harvard Business School, where my research focused on interpersonal communication and consumer psychology. Do you see what I did there? I subtly shifted the attention away from the institution and toward my research focus. And, of course, what I said is true. But it sounds very different [from] if I had just said I attended Harvard Business School." By shifting attention or providing more detail that you want others to focus on, you open up a bigger conversation.

## Fear of Being Obnoxious

The Bragging Rights research data shows that "being obnoxious" is *by far* the number one concern of those who fear self-promotion. Several people commented along the lines of "I worry about being seen as a used car salesman." So, please hear this: *If you're worried about being obnoxious, you're probably not obnoxious.* Some points to consider in this light:

- Are you a know-it-all?
- Are you overpromising and under-delivering?
- Are you putting anyone down or comparing?
- Are you feigning humility?
- Are you saying statements like "I am a genius"?
- Are you in love with your own voice?

- Do you ramble on without pausing for others to express their thoughts?
- Is the conversation always about you?

The tricky part is that we can't measure what is obnoxious because what sounds like "tooting your own horn" to one person is simply conversation to the next. A brag is only positive, negative, or neutral depending on who hears and interprets it. Some might not think anything of it because you are telling a story in context, you are sharing knowledge, or they've already accomplished it, so they know a similar journey.

As I've said, many of us feel a certain "ick factor" with bragging, and with all the conflicting norms around showing success, what people feel is acceptable varies. Your job is to learn how to do it in a way that serves you and those around you, by building your social currency. It's not vanity to share what you've done or are doing, because it is in service to others. But there are techniques for bragging that lend themselves to confidence as well as being socially palatable.

Muhammad Ali is attributed with saying "It's not bragging if you can back it up." Here's a hard truth: you can be the best in the world and have quantifiable information to prove it, but research shows that your audience likely won't care about the data. Dr. Amanda Nimon-Peters, a professor of leadership at Hult International Business School, studies influence. She discovered that "in one meta-analysis of forty-nine studies in the workplace involving close to 9,000 people, influencers who used rational persuasion were found to be successful only about 12 percent of the time."

Make your data tell a story. You will be more convincing if you make someone feel emotion when you talk about your success, achievements, or experiences. Use statements that capture emotion, such as ones that mention benefits people will care about. Keep your brag book updated with examples, case studies, stories, anecdotes, comments from others, and statistics and data you're allowed to collect and share. Know why you care about these things and why others should too.

## Traps to Avoid

Bragging means talking about your success with pride. But you must talk about that success with some strategy, especially if your win means someone else has fallen.

In late summer 2022, Lisa LaFlamme, an award-winning anchor of one of Canada's most popular newscasts on the CTV network, posted a video on Twitter announcing that she had been removed from her role. LaFlamme had been with the network for thirty-five years. In the video, she said she had been "blindsided" by the termination of her contract. Just fifty-one minutes after LaFlamme's post, her replacement, Omar Sachedina, posted on Twitter, "I am honoured to be following in the footsteps of Lisa LaFlamme and Lloyd Robertson. So excited to be working with our incredibly talented team in this new role!" (Robertson was LaFlamme's predecessor, who had retired twelve years earlier, at the age of seventy-seven.)

We labor over what to write or say in self-promotion tactics, but timing is just as critical. Whatever his intentions, Sachedina's ill-timed Tweet seemed self-aggrandizing. It made him look pompous as he celebrated while LaFlamme faced her shocking downfall. His credibility and the public's trust in him took a hit. The network management later wrote a press release regretting the timing of the announcements.

When you have good news to share, scan to see if the timing is right. Take a breath, let the person get off the elevator before you jump on your celebration, so to speak. Give it a few days or even weeks, or let other people tell the story. In any setting, the story will leak out. In this instance, I'm sure a decent reporter or two would have figured it out fast.

As I've stated already, bragging is celebrating your accomplishments, and self-promotion is putting bragging into action. But there are many other strategies for you to recognize. These are ones to avoid or use knowing context and potential risk.

## Inferiority and Superiority Complexes

Avoid "canceling" a brag or adding a qualifier; for example, "I'm not trying to brag, but I'm a genius." You'll also see "I hate to brag, but...." Just avoid saying anything like this. It draws attention to the fact that you're not comfortable with the success you've achieved and in an awkward "don't look at me, look at me" type of way.

Likewise, avoid self-superiority. Avoid phrases like "I'm the best," "I have the most expensive...." They reflect an exaggerated sense of self-worth. Often, a superiority complex is just feelings of inferiority in disguise. You've got to strike that balance of loving your work and talking about it while keeping a healthy perspective.

**Titles.** Titles are limited. You might have *positional* influence, where your power is attached to your title, but you will likely see that influence wane when you move away from that job. It's the position that has power, and it's about authority. No matter your role, you want to focus on having *professional* influence rather than flaunt your title. This type of influence carries with you. You'll have a more resilient professional influence when you've won hearts and minds.

When self-promoting,
take yourself to
fear plus 10 percent.

**Humblebragging.** Humblebragging sounds like a good compromise, and many people have taken to it, but it doesn't work. People can see right through it. A humblebrag is a complaint and a brag together. It's a self-critical statement that also has an achievement attached to it. It's a prime example of false modesty. It's far too contrived and inauthentic. People who use it want your attention and your sympathy. It is much better to be plain and brag or list your complaint alone, but don't combine them. Here's an example: "I'm so tired. It's exhausting being at the awards function. I'm so humbled that they picked me; the award is gorgeous." It usually accompanies a picture of someone who is dressed up holding the award. As a side note, don't use "humbled" in any award acceptances. You are worthy of the award. Adding "humbled" to a statement doesn't make it more diplomatic. It is so cliché now that it sounds insincere.

The word you want to use is "honored," which reflects appreciation for what has been given. Humblebragging can also sound innocent—for example: "I can't believe they picked me. I'm so not worthy." But that type of gripe about something other people desire will only annoy people. Think about the person who wasn't picked or the judges who chose you.

**FIGJAM.** This story is about the uber-wealthy, but you might be able to see it in other contexts too. Dee Dee Taylor Eustace works in luxury: she has an impressive portfolio career that includes designing the interiors of superyachts. Her work was shortlisted for the 2016 World Superyacht Award. At one superyacht show, she learned a new term: "There's a thing called FIGJAM: [it stands for] f*ck, I'm great, just ask me," she told me. "FIGJAM. A guy who works there said, 'Oh, look at all these people just FIGJAMing,' [and] you know it's a bunch of wealthy guys hanging out just saying how great they are to each other." They have the megaphone to each other's ear, bragging about their wealth. That's their culture. It's expected and likely acceptable internally, but outside the circle, it's a great example of why the audience matters.

**One-upmanship.** One-upmanship is the art or practice of outdoing someone else. It can be about anything. Earlier in this book, for example, Lola Akinmade Åkerström gave the example of one parent talking about the level of education their child has, and in response, another parent says their child has a higher level. Running parallel to this is "one-downmanship"—the race to the bottom, where you tell others how you are worse off than they are. It's self-deprecation. This is tricky to navigate because there are real victims.

**Self-deprecation.** Self-deprecation is often taken at face value, which means there are pitfalls for this personal put-down. In the Bragging Rights survey, more than half of the respondents said, "I have a habit of self-deprecation." In her Netflix special *Nanette*, comedian Hannah Gadsby gives a stunning monologue about the damage of self-deprecation: "Do you understand what self-deprecation means when it comes from someone who is already in the margins? It's not humility. It's humiliation. I put myself down in order to speak, in order to seek permission to speak." Women in general engage in self-deprecation all the time so as to appear nonthreatening and to fit in. When we're not in power, making ourselves the easy punchline, the need to excuse our own existence, keeps the joke on us. (More to come on this for those in leadership in chapter 13.)

**Moral grandstanding.** Moral grandstanding involves outdoing someone else's concern about a situation. It is an egotistical act that often involves a heightened sense of justice. It's easy to see on social media. We're worried how we look—that we don't seem as though we care as much about something as the next person, so then we up it, looking more outraged than we are. We rail against the unfairness of something, the audacity of someone, and go the extra mile in shaming others for behavior that is typically seen as wrong. "You're outraged? Well, I'm even more outraged! Off with her head!" Moral grandstanding has several negative consequences, including "outrage exhaustion."

**Underbragging.** The underbrag is the "I'm so great, I don't care what you think" brag. Think of the self-deprecating, (slightly) mortifying jokes told by many women in comedy shows. They often use the underbrag in humor—you might think of it as a way to stoop to conquer. Writer Jenn Doll coined the term after analyzing an Internet spree of humblebragging. Underbragging, she writes, is defined as "when you brag your own disaster or situation that one would not normally brag about." One example Doll shares is "I got dumped on a Post-it note!" (Perhaps here referencing an episode of TV show *Sex in the City* when Carrie blurts to her friends, "Berger broke up with me—*on a Post-it!*" and proceeds to go on about it, overshadowing her friend's engagement announcement moments before.)

**F*cked-up brags.** Closely related to the underbrag, "f*cked up brags" are part of a global movement where people get together to share how they've failed and commemorate their losses. One organization hosts events where three to four speakers, on stage for only seven minutes, share their stories of business and professional failures. The purpose is to help people realize that no one achieves success overnight (except for the highly privileged) and to learn from the mistakes. The group was formed in Mexico in 2012 while friends were out for drinks. One of the cofounders, Leticia Gasca, wondered why "everyone always talks about the Zuckerbergs and Gates[es] of the world, but no one shares candid stories of failures." The point is to celebrate instead of stigmatize failure. But while authenticity and transparency are important, this practice is easier done by those who have a level of privilege and likely a huge amount of success, so the f*ucked up brag is not much more than a tiny balancing act. If you go this route, make sure your seven minutes hold a heavy amount of context. See chapter 10 for a better way of telling your failure and redemption stories.

**Flexing.** Flexing is a term from social media that means showing off. It got its start at the gym, but now it also refers to showing off material possessions and wealth, physique, travel, and how intelligent you are. These types of posts require self-awareness and an understanding of your audiences. (We'll talk more about audiences in chapters 8 and 11.) Is it a badge for status, or is it your status?

**Stunts.** Notice-me stunts take self-promotion to the next level. This one takes us back to 1997, but it's a great one: Uisok Hwang, a self-described "investor and Internet specialist" from Seoul, South Korea, took out an ad of himself casually standing next to the text "Masayoshi Son, I'd like to meet you!" He was interested in catching the attention of only one person, Son, who is a Korean-Japanese billionaire who runs mobile and telecom investment giant SoftBank Group.

The stunt got him half a page in the *New York Times Magazine*: "Hwang, 34, affably admits he was worried that his ad made him look like a clown, but as he puts it, 'There is no kind of idiot who would spend $10,000 just for a joke.' Son must have agreed. Soon after the ad ran, Son agreed to meet Hwang at the Seoul airport. No deals were cut, but Son did share his coveted E-mail address, which Hwang will use to pitch his ideas for world domination."

## Don't Worry about It!

The answer to worries about being rejected or annoying while self-promoting is ultimately "Don't worry about it." Boom. Simple. Here's the longer answer: if you worry about being rejected or annoying, it becomes a self-fulfilling prophecy. A study on the workplace at the University of British Columbia found that while it's normal for people to wonder if they're liked, if they worry about such things, they'll seek out the information to confirm their fears. It will annoy their colleagues and increase the likelihood that they will be rejected or subverted.

You can be more pleasant and delightful by sharing your wisdom and experiences with others, but to do it with grace and ease, you need intention and that's what we'll cover in the next chapter.

## ••• Bragging Right •••

Stretch beyond the boundaries of your comfort zone. When self-promoting, take yourself to fear plus 10 percent. This means taking yourself a tad outside your comfort zone (where your brain starts to say, *Oh no, not you*), then going even further—reaching for that bolder action. It's the same formula you should use when pricing your own work, because, like so many of us, you likely undervalue yourself.

Instead of mining your past for all your brag-worthy items, consider what you are doing today. Make it about right now and liberate yourself from having to go back into your vault of past successes. Mine the gems as you move forward. And when you have something you want to share, share it.

**To Consider:** Are you trying to impress people or are you sharing an experience that is important, captivating, or special? Is it knowledge that shares wisdom, skills, or experiences so that others can learn?

**To Do:** List twenty of your work successes. These don't have to be hardcore facts that have data behind them. These are your truths from your viewpoint. Think about accomplishments, steps of courage, and contributions. What outcomes did you have for yourself, your team, or the goals of your organization? What was the impact? What did you learn from each success?

**To Share:** What sounds like bragging to one person is just a conversation to another. Share this fact with a friend.

# 8

# Brag with Purpose

WE ARE famous for expecting people to know what we want. We think and say things like, "Isn't it obvious that I should get that client?" "Isn't it obvious I should get that new opportunity?" "How could they not know how desperately I want that promotion?"

But people are much better mind readers when they know your vision. They need to know your general direction, not your road map, so they can help you.

This is no longer a time to keep all your options open. Closing some doors will make this work more effective. You'll need to set constraints on what you want to be known for (not everything), who you want to be known by (not everyone), and what you're going to talk about (not everything).

Your vision is where you want to go, where you see yourself in the future. Because life has so many twists and turns, I find it's best not to fixate on an exact position but instead on a direction. It's a journey of your professional career, beyond any one single title. If all things lined up, way down the horizon, what would it look like? What's your vision?

Let's predict your future.

## Vision

Where would you like to see yourself in the long term—three, five, ten years from now? Your vision will guide your self-promotion work such that you align your goals with your vision and then your tactics behind your goals.

Answer these questions to help you figure out your vision:

- What does a better world look like to you?
- What are you trying to achieve?
- What do you want to be known for?
- If you became known as the world's go-to expert on any topic, what would that be?
- How are you going to create value for yourself and others?

Review your answers. What ties them together? What you'll start to see is your position. Know that you can position yourself or be positioned. You can own your story, or someone will make up a story or simply ignore you.

## Audience Matters

When I started MediaFace, I said, "We can work with anyone!" The reality was we couldn't. We weren't into lifestyle work or commercials. We needed healthy but not exorbitant budgets. We ultimately had to decide who we were best going to serve. Doing so helped those who were looking for our services pre-qualify themselves, and it saved us and them a lot of time.

The insight is that one-third of people will like or love you, one-third will be indifferent, and, sorry to say, the final third won't like you at all. Most of us are wired to fixate on those who don't like us. We remember the sting of the rejection much more than the yes, the boo more than the applause. Most of us are wired to want to be liked; we have been since childhood. As an adult, you don't need to chase the people who aren't inclined toward you. Build your relationships with those who already like you. That will be enough. They'll help attract others to you.

When I was working in content creation, people would ask me, "How long should my videos be?" "What's the best word count for a magazine article [or blog post]?" "What's the best length for a podcast?" But length is irrelevant. Think about it this way: if something isn't for you, you probably won't spend five seconds watching or reading or listening to it. But if it is for you, you might watch or read or listen to it for hours. (Have you binge-watched anything lately?) MediaFace made a mathematics series that was three hours long. People watched it and they read the transcripts. The audience was not huge, but for those it mattered to, it *really* mattered. They were raving fans and spread the word. The videos on the site won an award, and then we had people visit us from all over the world asking us about the website and the series. We made work for people who cared and they told their peers. Even though the site is gone, we still get emails from people asking about it. They miss it. Will people miss your message when you're gone?

You can't be for everyone—that's exhausting. But you can be for some. And you must be relevant to the people you matter most to. To figure out your smallest viable audience, ask yourself these questions:

- Who am I for?
- Who do I want to talk to?
- Why do I want to talk to them?

- Why is this audience important to me right now?
- What does success look like?
- What have I achieved?

When considering your audience, you can think about fields of visibility, as in particular arenas of influence—in-field, wide-field, and off-field.

You might want to be visible within your office or company. This is **in-field** visibility, where you target self-promotion to internal audiences such as other leaders, the C-suite, your team, and interest groups. When we started working together, Neela White wanted to be the rock star of her unit. She wanted to be the go-to person in geriatrics for the financial services firm where she is a partner. She now gives presentations, is featured in corporate communications, and speaks at the firm's national event to a packed room (which has led to more opportunities).

**Wide-field** visibility means working for social currency in your larger industry or neighboring sectors. Here, your objective is to be known by associations, vendors, and leaders at competing companies within the industry. Jennifer Hayman owns a landscape design firm. Her goal is to be seen and heard within her industry, as she envisions partnerships that could benefit her in the future. She's already won many major regional awards for her designs. That gives her some clout as she contacts the people she's decided are influencers, to make sure they know her. She's also dedicated a portion of her social media posts directly to interior designers, who often look for people with Hayman's expertise for collaborations.

When you want to go broader, to external audiences, that's **off-field.** You're working to be in the mainstream media and to make alliances and associations in other industries. International conferences, for example, fit the bill and bring a wide range of people together.

By trying to appeal to everyone, you appeal to no one. Instead of broadcasting, think of "narrowcasting."

Choosing a field to focus on is critical. If you think you *should* talk to everyone but don't have the capacity, you will likely talk to no one. I don't want that for you. Global companies can afford to talk to everyone. But you are not a mega-brand like Coca-Cola, Nike, or Apple. They have the teams, the in-depth psychographics, and the budgets. If you try to talk to everyone, you'll have a hard time connecting with anyone.

To help you focus, think about purposeful visibility. Again, ask yourself:

- Who do I want to talk to?
- Why are they important to me?
- Do I want an in-field, wide-field, or off-field audience for the next three months?

If you're talking to the wrong audience, your wisdom and achievements don't matter. Consider your primary, secondary, and tertiary audiences. Review your social channels, networks, associations, contact list, and other relationships. Who are you giving your time to right now? Who will benefit you in the future? Who will give you opportunities in the future? Who should be relegated to the sidelines? Who are the critics that just don't count? Whose sun do you need to be in? Which relationships can you leverage? When a family member is part of the criticism, ask yourself, Is this person in the position I want to be in?

Your audience will change throughout the years. The audience you had when you began your career isn't necessarily the audience you want for the future. You don't have to drop them, but you'll want to focus your efforts on whom you want to attract in the future. Older audiences might not align with where you want to go.

## Brand Promise

After determining your vision and audience, you can set a brand promise. A brand promise is simply a statement so people can understand what you do and whom you serve. As I explained in chapter 1, it's what people say about you when you're not in the room. Your brand promise is what will take you to the future. It's not based on your reputation or your past. It projects where you are going.

It doesn't have to be fancy; in fact, it is best to make it as plain as possible. For example:

I help _____[my audience]_____ do _____[the action/result]_____.

My example is: *I help leaders [my audience] to be seen and heard [the action/result]*.

That's a start, but it would be better if I drilled down a bit more on whom I help: *I help high-achieving women be seen and heard*.

Eventually, I can swap out "help" for a different, more specific word: *I guide high-achieving women toward being seen and heard*.

Do you see how this statement has a benefit baked into it? Whatever you say or do, people want to know how it applies to them. When I was in TV news, we constantly challenged ourselves with the "so what?" test. So what does this matter? So what does this have to do with me? When you talk about benefits to your audience, you'll win them over.

So what's in it for you? You might want more trust, credibility, opportunities, a promotion, more quality clients, to be top of mind, and to have more people say yes to you with little effort. Answer the question for yourself. For me, it's that I am passionate about this work, and I want more opportunities to serve you and people like you. That lights me up and keeps me going.

● ● ●

# "The audience has always been my best director."

**EARTHA KITT**

## A Word about Intention

Megan, a senior vice president in financial services, was doing a lot to self-promote—on social, on TV—but she realized that she was like a pinball. Her self-promotion was like a part-time job that wasn't bringing in any income. During a one-to-one mentoring session with me, she confided that she wasn't getting the traction she expected.

Megan was a super-achiever—highly successful and driven. She had media opportunities and was often called on as an expert guest on panels, morning TV, and business TV, which she had been doing for years. The opportunities had given her great social proof. Her colleagues would often send her notes saying things like, "Caught you on the show, great job." She liked the quick ego boost but still felt drained afterward, and she didn't know why it all felt sort of meaningless and rote.

I wanted to know, What did she really want? What was all of this for? To get at the answer, we did an exercise that goes seven layers deep. You can do it by yourself. I suggest audio-recording your answers for simplicity, but writing them down works too. Here's how it goes:

- Ask yourself, "What's my intention? What do I want?" Record your answer.

- Then ask, "What will that do for me?" Again, record your answer.

- Repeat and answer "What will that do for me?" five more times. (Resist the temptation to give up after three rounds.)

The exercise sounds deceptively easy. But you won't get near the truth until you've responded to the question "What will that do for me?" four or five times. If you can do this with a partner to help you dig deep, it's a great bonding experience.

What's the intention? Peel it back and ask yourself, "What do I want? Why do I want to do this?" Once you peel back from the fancy and fun, what you want is likely much more meaningful. Megan realized that she really wanted to have more trust with her teams. I asked, "What will that do for you?"

"I'll feel more like I belong," she said.

Megan found that her real intention was to make her mark with those already connected to her. She wanted a more profound sense of belonging. That deeper sense of belonging wasn't going to be found in media appearances. So that cleared the way for her to be more strategic about her self-promotion approach. She wrote to me to say that she'd set a goal to get to know more team members at different levels and was going to start a tour of North America. The communications team was happy because they were going to have a camera at select locations so she could interview her colleagues and team members.

This wasn't the first time I heard people say they were professionally lonely so they planned to self-promote to make real relationships that stick.

Your intention behind every effort of self-promotion matters. If you feel a heightened sense of angst when you self-promote, think of the reason you're doing it or remember that you're doing it for the benefit of others. But not everyone is your audience.

I'm not for everyone; you're not for everyone. As I've said, by trying to appeal to everyone, you appeal to no one. Instead of broadcasting, think of "narrowcasting." When you're talking to the right audience, you'll notice your bragging and self-promotion working better. You won't feel cluttered. Your mind will wander less when you are not distracted by considering every possibility, and you'll have more energy to move forward on your goals. For example, Dr. Jacqueline Kerr no longer considers her parents as part of her audience. (This happens more than you think.) In an interview, she told me, "I would share with my parents that I'd done a television interview, and I'd tell my dad to watch it," but eventually she stopped because he always gave negative feedback. "He'd say, 'Oh, you say, "um" a lot.' It just broke me, to be honest, because I just wasn't ever enough." Kerr is in the top 1 percent of cited scientists worldwide. Her parents were simply not her ideal audience. Cutting out the need for approval by people who aren't your intended audience means you won't waste time and mental energy. It's foundational to purposeful self-promotion.

## • • • Bragging Right • • •

What do you really want to create? What's the point, deep down? Getting clear on it now will make a difference in your direction and make whatever you do feel rewarding and worthwhile. When you bring the right message to the right person at the right time in a way that causes them to think differently, you create real connections.

**To Consider:** What's your legacy? Think of yourself at the surprising age of 130. You're able to do so much more without the constraints of our current time frames. You're sitting under a tree telling the story of your life to your family and friends. What are the stories you're telling them?

**To Do (a):** Did you skip the Vision exercise at the beginning of the chapter? Do it! Then mark your calendar to review it in three months to make sure you're on track.

**To Do (b):** Instead of choosing a quote from the same old suspects to post on social media channels, grab the extraordinary words of a friend or colleague and repost them, giving them credit. It will make someone's day, and you'll be a thought leader curating new and different viewpoints instead of a follower rehashing the same content everyone else posts.

**To Share:** Tell a friend: the age of broadcasting is over. Narrowcasting allows you to focus on the people you are meant to serve. The smallest viable audience will appreciate you and invite others.

# 9

# Know What Makes You Remarkable

JOE FOSTER'S story should be legendary. He took a small shoe company he had founded with his brother and made it a household name. He's the thrust behind Reebok. His success skyrocketed when he took the then $9 million company from the UK into the US market. Four years later, it was worth $900 million—thanks to his success in the women's market. Reebok was the first fitness shoe designed and developed for women's feet, and early influencers like Jane Fonda flocked to buy them during the aerobics craze.

But when Foster decided to search for his name online in later years, he found stories that were wrong or vastly incomplete. He hadn't curated his stories or considered the online legacy potential that sharing his knowledge could offer for generations. Foster said, "I was brought up in a world of the remarkably average, where aspiring to be better was frowned upon. It was an era of 'know your place,' 'don't rock the boat,' and other edicts injected into the masses to keep society in order... Decency was paramount... alongside respect for others. But in my mind, contrary to societal expectations, so was growth and improvement through challenging myself."

At eighty-six years old, Foster decided to set the record straight by writing his autobiography, *Shoemaker: The Untold Story of the British Family Firm That Became a Global Brand.*

During his book launch at Zvelle, a Canadian shoe store, I asked him about setting the story straight, and he said, "You need to own your own story." By doing so and telling people what he did and is doing, Foster is mentoring even more young shoemakers, like Elle AyoubZadeh, the founder of Zvelle, and inspiring generations to challenge themselves. He recognizes, embraces, and promotes what distinguishes him from other business owners of his day, adding his perspective and living his values.

Foster has the right idea too: "Some people run to beat others. I ran to beat myself."

You now know whom you want to serve. The next step is to know why they should want to listen to you. What is it about your story that needs to be heard? Why are you the authority? Gain clarity on your story so that you are the signal and not just part of the noise. Telling your own story allows you to showcase what you think makes you remarkable.

What makes you, you? Your answer to that question may not make sense to anyone else. It can be tangible and intangible, and it can be more about a felt quality than how you appear to others.

Most of us want both to be valued as individuals and to belong. Social psychologists call this optimal distinctiveness theory. We want to be associated with a group identity (part of X team, X company, X school, or X experience) but also need to be seen for what makes us unique. Basically, we want to stand out and fit in.

You have multiple identities that are interwoven. You are still a parent when you go to work. Your professional life is in your home life, and you can't just sever the two. Your professional identity isn't your job title or where you are today in your career. My own sense of identity was once very bound to my role. I was the CEO. Then I realized: it's not the title; it's wisdom, skills,

Position yourself as *different*, embrace your weirdness, and distinguish yourself from what others are doing. Set yourself apart as *relevant*, connecting to conversations that matter.

and all the lessons learned. A title gives you a uniform, but your identity enhances it. You are more fluid than your title, but you may get caught on it when signaling your identity to the world. You don't have to limit yourself to showing up in the world one way at a time. You can use everything. You get to choose how you want to show up in your self-promotion. Some clients choose to share pictures of their family on trips or integrate their pets into their professional lives. You don't have to keep your life compartmentalized if you feel comfortable sharing. In a moment, we'll add some constraints around what you talk about, but know that people want to know you beyond your title.

## You Are Remarkable

How are you remarkable? Most people can write about how their children, friends, or colleagues are remarkable, but many people struggle to answer it about themselves.

Right now, take ten minutes and think of ways you are remarkable. You could start with "I am remarkable because . . ." If you can write down your reasons, that's even better. Leave the paper in your top drawer or somewhere you will spot it when you need it. Use these questions as a prompt:

- What is unusual about me?
- What surprises me?
- What impresses me?
- What are my achievements?
- What makes me fascinating?
- What accomplishments should I share?

This information will start to reveal what makes you remarkable. Use the results to craft a bio or in anything new that you're about to write for your self-promotion. It's also a great list to inspire you to write social content. If you're doing any media, including podcasts, be able to answer these questions. Make an electronic copy of your answers and put them in a folder labeled "Remarkable Me" on your computer desktop.

And note "remarkable" doesn't mean "better"—which is a competitive stance. That word also renders descriptions transactional—as in cheaper, faster, how good, how many—encouraging people to compare you directly to someone else. Instead, help people see you as someone offering an experience to work with you, or transformations that no one else could help bring about. There's only one of you. Give yourself permission to position yourself as *different*, embrace your weirdness, and distinguish yourself from what others are doing. Set yourself apart as *relevant*, connecting to conversations that matter.

## Know Your Superpowers

Some people call them "specialized abilities"; some, your "core competencies." I call them superpowers. Knowing who you are at your core will help you differentiate yourself from others and give you stories you can brag about. Let's figure out your superpowers.

1. List three things that make you stand out from your peers.
2. List three skills you've developed that make you successful at what you do.
3. List two things in your business that make you the happiest and that you'd never outsource, or two things in your job that you would never delegate.

"In order to stand out, we first have to know what we stand for."

**SIMON SINEK**

4 Write down two to three stories about turning points in your professional journey—your epiphany moments or transformational points. (For example, when did the carpet get pulled out from underneath you? Did you get fired from a job? Did you decide to do your own thing? Take a relationship to another level? These are moments that you didn't necessarily see coming.)

5 Think back to when you were twelve years old. What would you say to your younger self? What would they say to you about your journey and all you've accomplished?

6 What's the traditional background of influential people in your field? How are you different from them? How can you leverage these differences?

We often get caught up listening to other voices, but we need to pause to listen to our own voice to make sure we're on the right path, the one that matters to us. Stopping to reflect helps us move forward faster because we can ensure we're on our authentic path. Have a trusted confidant work with you on what makes you different or remarkable.

## Passion, Enthusiasm, and Grit

I'm a passionate person. If there's something I'm interested in, I'm all in. That devotion has opened doors for me: I've earned new business and won several prizes as a result of commenting on a conference's social media while sitting in the audience. I was added to the meet-and-greet additional social event by the hosts when I connected with them before the event. Saying thank you and letting hosts and sponsors know my key takeaway from an event has also given me more business connections. (You can do it in person or in an email or social post.)

You can decide to be passionate or at least enthusiastic about what makes you who you are too. If you want to be a leader, expert, or visionary, you must share your enthusiasm with others. People appreciate when you share in this way and are often eager to offer support. Passion builds empires. Next time you're with someone, ask them to tell you something they're passionate about. You'll notice their eyes light up, and the words come tumbling out.

Here are some prompts for you to consider when determining your passion:

- Have you completed any side projects that really excited you?
- What makes your eyes light up?
- What can you show instead of tell?

Enthusiasm is a hidden tool of self-promotion. So go ahead and express it. Get a little heated and rant for five minutes. Wax poetic about something or someone you love. People are drawn to people with deeply held convictions. In the end, you'll be able to see that you are, indeed, passionate about something. Be enthusiastic. Most people don't want to come across as "highly emotional," so you'll stand out with little effort—but in a good way!

Author and researcher Liz Wiseman also has found that passion is relevant to making you a remarkable businessperson in your field. In their article "Impact Players of the Workplace" Wiseman and her coauthor, Lauren Hancock, found that impact players—whom they define as "those indispensable colleagues who can be counted on in critical situations and who consistently receive high-profile assignments and new opportunities"—channel their energy, strengths, and passion into how they go about their work rather than into the type of work they do. No matter what your role is, you'll make the greatest impact by including and expressing passion in your approach.

Grit is part of our passion and enthusiasm. It's the perseverance to be consistent and commit. You need grit to make it day in and day out of doing self-promotion and building it into a practice. Athletes, high-profile leaders, artists, and writers, for example, become successful when they consistently adhere to their workouts, goals, and schedules no matter the struggle. Grit helps them exert maximum effort and see the goal beyond any short-term wins or negative feedback.

## Answers Change

Our visions of success, passion, and purpose change. We can't help it. We're collecting new information all the time. Peter Drucker, who was a well-known management consultant and author, "liked to tell the story of the man who attends his 40-year college reunion and sees his former professor just as he is about to administer a final exam. The old grad looks at the test and says, 'Professor Smithers, these are the same questions you asked us 40 years ago!' Smithers nods and says, 'Yes, but the answers are different.'

"'We always thought it was a joke. No—this is wisdom,' Drucker explained. 'The answers to questions do not remain the same . . . You learn to do a little better, to push back that infinite boundary of ignorance just a bit.'"

The point is it's okay to pivot and change how you show up. The intention is that you contribute, perform, and serve your value. That you feel fulfilled. The more you think about how remarkable you truly are, the more you'll truly believe it. Keep asking the important questions about what makes you remarkable. In the next chapter, I'll share how to start telling others about just that.

### ••• Bragging Right •••

What irreplaceable difference do you offer? Discovering this will make you feel more fulfilled. You will eventually change direction—that's a given because you keep learning and growing—but you already have a vast amount of knowledge to share with the world.

**To Consider:** What makes you precious, remarkable, valuable, or important? What are your passions? What comes easily to you? Go beyond "I'm funny," "I'm organized," or "I'm a hard worker." Make it more specific, meaningful, and descriptive.

**To Do (a):** Search for yourself online. Do the search results reflect the story you want to tell? Do you have a story online? Update your content with your superpower information. What you put out there today will become part of your story.

**To Do (b):** Consider your values. What do you hold most dear? Listen to that whisper in your head telling you whether or not to care about something. It helps you prioritize the choices in your professional life. If your first answers are "honesty," "compassion," or "trust," go deeper. You want to get past the easy, automatic answers that everyone expects from you. If honesty, for example, is a core value, dig into the word to understand why it really matters to you.

**To Share:** Share with a networking group the importance of being enthusiastic. Prompt someone to talk about something they are passionate about, and then read from the "Passion, Enthusiasm, and Grit" section above.

# 10

# Own Your Knowledgeable Authority

I'VE "SWORN IN" hundreds of experts. I've given certificates, held my daughter's magic wand, and other times, for more effect, wielded a lightsaber. To get to this swearing-in part of my program, the "experts-to-be" tell me or their table partners a short story of success. It's often a fun part of the workshop. These people, of course, are already leaders, experts, and visionaries; they are already enough. They just need someone to help take away the doubt and fears. They need someone else to validate the idea that they are enough so they can fully believe it themselves. Leaders, experts, and visionaries are made, not born.

There's something for every level in this chapter, but I am aiming for you to claim your title as expert for yourself, even if you never utter the words "I'm an expert." (Yes, you are now; say it again in your head.)

The CEOs, entrepreneurs, and high-achieving go-getters I've sworn in, like you, aren't people looking for a get-expert-status-quick type of fakery. They haven't just read three books and watched a TED Talk. They aren't just one or two steps ahead of the people they lead, serve, coach, and consult. They are people, like Deirdre, who need to be heard. She had already consulted with people who work at the global level. She had two degrees along with certificates that could wallpaper an office. She was already an expert, but she treated herself like a hidden gem, having believed the big lie that she had to wait for someone to tell her she was an expert. Otherwise, she thought she would be obnoxiously claiming a title that wasn't hers. In truth, everyone saw her as an expert, but no one bothered to say it to her.

Like Deirdre, we often fear bragging because we haven't gathered our thoughts around what we want to say. We're quick to diminish our own genius and credibility because we haven't put a stake in the ground to support our vision. There's also that faint concern that someone will demand that we prove what we know (which won't happen) and a nagging voice that might say, *Why should anyone listen to me?* Overcoming this requires advance planning and vision. Because you are already an expert, you can make yourself the authority simply by deciding what you want to be known for.

To begin, you need to learn to tune into your internal authority. Authoring your own life is freeing. You can ground yourself in your values and be more responsible for where, why, and how you move through life. Ask yourself these questions:

- Do you know when you've done a good job or wait for others to tell you?

- Do you wait for others to celebrate you, or do you celebrate yourself?

- Do you sweep your achievements aside because no one noticed them?

Anchor yourself with a simple question: "What do you think?" Ask yourself this regularly and often, and especially when you may be at risk of defaulting to an external authority. Then consider your next steps based on your internal thinking.

You can be influential simply by having a point of view and articulating it.

- You can be a **knowledge broker**, where you curate ideas from other people with a central theme to your curation. You sometimes put your spin on the information. You're ahead of others on what's new. Often, leaders are knowledge brokers.

- An **expert** is someone who develops their own content and thought leadership, and when they share others' work, they always add their own opinions.

- A **visionary** sees around corners, or into the future, and communicates a distinct vision. They might take something controversial (like "bragging is a good thing") and add a perspective.

You don't have to articulate which one you are to the world, but know in your mind how you want to be seen. All are great and you may be a visionary in most of your work and simultaneously a knowledge broker in something you're interested in.

And as we discussed earlier, don't feel that you have to roll out your qualifications, achievements, or status when you tell people what you know. You can weave in your social proof if you need to, but if someone is curious, they'll look you up.

## Riff Tool

The best self-promotion isn't you with an award (but I do like to see it); it's you sharing the knowledge you've accumulated along your professional journey. We often don't realize how much we know or consider the successes we've had along the way. I hear it over and over again: "I don't know what to say or talk about." This simple tool along with three to twenty minutes will banish that concern. It will take you even further if you have the vision you set for yourself at the front of your mind (see chapter 8). Here's how it goes:

1. Set a timer for three minutes and write down as fast as you can what you like to talk about. What do you care about? Here are some starter prompts to get you going:

   - I believe...
   - I like talking about...
   - I could teach the world/the nation/my colleagues/my friends how to...
   - The biggest needle mover for me was...
   - The biggest mistake I made was...
   - The best habit I have is...
   - No one else knows this, but...

2. Look at the list. Circle or group items together.

3. Identify the commonalities or throughlines.

Those throughlines are things you should talk about and share. On the next level, what could you easily talk about for twenty minutes? Turn on your microphone and record a conversation with yourself. Then, using speech-to-text or transcription tools, produce a text version. One of my mentors used this technique to write magazine articles that he turned into a book. You've just discovered what you should be sharing as self-promotion and a whole lot of content ideas for you to use in the future. To be stronger, add a point of view.

## Your Point of View

Knowing your point of view conveys that you're a person on a mission. When you can articulate a problem, people see you as the person who can solve it for them. They see you as the solution. Have you ever thought about yourself as a solution?

Author Seth Godin noted that a point of view is "the difference between saying, 'What would you like me to do,' and 'I think we should do this, not that.' A point of view is the difference between a job and a career. It's the difference between being a cog and making an impact. Having a point of view is different from always being correct. No one is always correct. Hiding because you're not sure merely makes you invisible." Expressing your point of view conditions your audience to see you a certain way—as the leader, the expert, the visionary, the person who is ready for a huge promotion or for a larger account or for a next-level client.

So how do you develop your point of view? You don't need to know everything about what you care about; you just need to curate and communicate a consistent view of your vision. What is your opinion on what you care about? What's your big idea? Do you know of a better way to do something? What experiences have you had that others likely haven't? Having a distinct point of view where fewer people are playing can help. What knowledge can you bring from the rest of the world to your hometown? How can you be the local expert? How are you different from the traditional or influential people in your field? Could the fact that you're an outlier be a feature? Do you have a model you could share?

I used to be a videographer, so I would shoot and edit my stories as well as report and appear in them. It's unglamorous. But I learned a lot about perspective from that job. When people told me how they saw the world, gave me their perspective, I could point my lens at it and share it with others. It would be a perspective I wouldn't have seen otherwise because I am tall or white or female, or because I haven't seen the world through their experience. There is only one of you who has the exact combination of experiences and identity you carry. Your perspective is a powerful tool.

## Pillars

Pillars are themes that carry your vision and point of view. And for the purposes of self-promotion, you are allowed only three pillars. Being contained and focused is necessary so that others will clearly see who you are, what you stand for, and how you serve. It makes you more captivating. Your pillars are the central themes that reflect you. Which themes already run through your professional life? What connects, expresses, or illustrates you at the core?

I was working with Phil, a VP in a Fortune 200 company, who didn't want to lead from a strictly analytical position (the head); he also wanted to appeal to the heart and the gut. Phil discovered his pillars are:

- **Trust (gut):** "I'm committed to helping others in a dedicated way."

- **Future (head):** "The future is here. I'll help everyone evolve with the technology."

- **Care (heart):** "I value and care about my team. Each of them is vital to our success."

Expressing your point of view conditions your audience to see you a certain way—as the leader, the expert, the visionary, the person who is ready.

Every time Phil sends a message out as part of his self-promotion, he considers these three pillars. They are broad but are the first step for him. They help him remember what he wants to convey and nurture.

When your pillars are solid, people can easily recognize them. They show up without guessing and are reliable for you and the audience. The "head, heart, gut" rubric is useful to frame your three pillars, but it's not the only way. For instance, Jenn Harper, founder and CEO of Cheekbone Beauty, has these three pillars: sustainability, Indigenous community, and beauty. Her messages in interviews, posts, and profiles always forefront these three themes.

Let's put this all together by looking at my point of view and pillars, starting with my brand promise. Remember, that is:

> I guide high-achieving women toward
> being seen and heard.

My point of view is that hidden gems need to be seen and heard; we can't wait for others to give us permission, and we need to change the system that tells some to wait until they are chosen.

My pillars are success, leadership, and women in business. I send out messages that relate to these three pillars through a range of tactics. On social media, for example, I write about how to talk about your success, and you'll also see me give points where I share others' successes and cheerlead them.

In my podcast, *Bold(h)er*, I talk about leadership and the challenges and successes of leaders who are in corporate and small business. Not everything is obvious. I do more behind the scenes, and you already do too. I show up in communities that help women succeed in business. I walk the talk.

Review your results of the Riff Tool questions you did earlier (see page 155) and look for themes. Write down the major ones and then keep working with them until you whittle them down to three that stick. Work with these pillars for at least six months. After you have your pillars for a while, you can drill down even more. Allow them to evolve over time.

Once your content is connected to your brand promise, you have a touchstone to anything you consider producing. People will start to recognize you for what you know if you keep it consistent.

## Your Story Bank

Let's get something out of the way first: do not bother developing an elevator pitch. It's just too much work that almost always goes sideways. We often get so lost in making it perfect that if we start to blurt it out and then slip up a word or two, we get off track and stumble. It's also too staged of a statement to just casually say when you encounter someone. Often, elevator pitches don't take context into account. It's a "here's what I *need* to tell you"—and *go*, stopwatch at the ready. It's cliché. So often, I've seen people get so rigid in "here's what I say and how I say it" that they miss the opportunity to have others see themselves in their story. You need to introduce yourself in a way that helps people connect with you, to have a brief conversation that makes the other person interested in having another conversation. That's the point of self-promotion.

Storytelling can help you connect with people. It inspires them as they feel or imagine that they can do something. They also might feel part of the process, especially if you update the story for them later. The stories we tell often define who we'll become—you are the hero of your own story.

As a reporter, I had a bank of stories that weren't dated that I could use in a certain season or for a specific reason. Some would be half-started or just a few words. Now, I give a workshop called "Shameless Storytelling" in which I help people develop a story bank unique to them.

I encourage you to develop one too. A story bank helps your mind start thinking of stories, and you'll have the beginnings of some go-to stories that you can use repeatedly. These go-to story ideas will mean you're not hunting for a story the day before a presentation. It means you'll be able to make deeper connections faster with some back-pocket stories when you meet people. Often, these stories stick more too.

When Karen Eber and I met, we instantly clicked. She's an author, leadership consultant, and speaker and was in the audience when I gave my TED Talk. She's a storyteller and has her own TED Talk, which has millions of views. It's fascinating. Eber gives this advice regularly: "We create interest by telling stories. Not by waiting for people to ask us to tell them." It's great advice. No one telling a story at your meetings? Here's your opportunity: *you* can. In her TED Talk, Eber says, "Storytelling is such a critical skill for a leader because the very act of telling a story makes people trust you more."

## Stories of Success

People like hearing stories of success. You're seen as more likeable if you tell stories of growth, communion, and agency. These stories allow you to craft a positive identity.

In precarious times, or in workplaces that are known to be insecure (like in media, where most jobs are like balloons at the mercy of many intensifying winds), keeping your success front and center is important. In TV newsrooms, the maxim most of us are trained to live by is that you're only as good as your last story. You can swap "story" for "result" or "deal." The idea is to keep egos in check, but business functions on short-term memory. Your stakeholders (bosses, clients, employees) are focused on what you can do for them right now. All that good in the past becomes very fluid, forgotten, and doesn't quite mean as much a week, two months, or a year later. You must keep your success stories alive and ready to tell.

One success story formula goes from a challenge (struggle) to action (turning point or solution) to outcome (good news, success in meeting a goal). Another is a simple "before and after" example. Yet another is the story of a lesson learned. Take a story from Mordy Golding, who is a group product manager at LinkedIn. Golding's best strategy presentation was a complete failure. After preparing to the max, and at the final hour before a presentation, he delivered what he thought was a killer performance, but the presentation fell flat. When he asked the CEO what went wrong, she said he had been too polished. "Lesson learned," Golding wrote. "You have to give your audience something to latch onto. You have to show where you want others to weigh in so that they feel they have part ownership in it too... Sometimes, being too good can be bad."

It wasn't that Golding's slides were too perfect; it was that he didn't leave room for others. But in this lesson learned, he portrays himself in such a great light. Even his last line—"sometimes, being too good can be bad"—points to his strengths.

## Villains to Heroes

People also like redemption stories. They score highly as attracting people's interest, which might be because the US media plays such a strong part of storytelling in the world, and they use that style all the time.

"Play long-term games with long-term people. All returns in life, whether in wealth, relationships, or knowledge, come from compound interest."

**NAVAL RAVIKANT**

A redemption story could be about how you lost your job but then rallied to build your empire. It could be that you flunked math, then became a wildly successful wealth advisor. Or it could be that you had a legal case against you, but you were able to pivot and reinvent (like my story about the big manila envelope I received at the beginning of this book). Consider, too, that if you're a high achiever, you're likely seen as both a villain and a hero from the lens of different perspectives. We're all flawed characters. Owning and sharing your redemption stories helps you to own your narrative, even when stories are less than flattering. Research shows that those who tell redemptive stories are judged as more likeable. The storytelling style is used best when you're in a position of power and influence.

Writer Julie Beck in *The Atlantic* shares, "The redemption story is American optimism—things will get better!—and American exceptionalism—I can make things better!—and it's in the water, in the air, and in our heads. This is actually a good thing a lot of the time. Studies have shown that finding a positive meaning in negative events is linked to a more complex sense of self and greater life satisfaction."

Telling our stories is important to connect with audiences, including your team, stakeholders, and on social media. It's how we learn from and bond with each other. It's how people find relatable role models—like you.

## Self-Mythology

If your story isn't working for you, tell a new story. Find a better story. Stories don't have to be facts; they are about *your* truth. I just don't recommend excessively exaggerating. As a young journalist, I realized that people would tell me a combination of fact, truth, and some self-mythology. With self-mythology, you are your primary character, so you craft stories about yourself as part of your own sense of significance and identity. You can change your interpretation of your personal stories as you like and as you evolve. You hold the keys to how you interpret your circumstances.

## Personal Professional Stories

People connect to personal professional stories. These are your professional stories with a personal slant, so they include you or someone close to you at the heart of the story. Some examples include your first-job stories, advice for the world of work from an elder, or achieving any personal goal. (Did you walk to the top of a mountain or bake a cake to feed a hundred people?) Here's an example of a story I posted in the summer of 2022 on LinkedIn. It featured a picture of a tiny tomato, just a little larger than a quarter:

> This is my $30 tomato.
> 
> Sometimes we plant seeds that take off and bring us a bounty. Other times, we spend $30 on plants and seeds and get one teeny, tiny tomato (that my daughter said was "dry").
> 
> As I write my book, *Bragging Rights*, I'm well aware that I might be spending a HUGE amount of time on something that might not, well, bear fruit. But it did allow me to get messy, cultivate my ideas, and gave me room to grow.
> 
> Hope your tomatoes are overflowing this year.

Our personal professional stories can also be our most relatable ones—where we show some of our ugly parts and make the audience gasp and say, "It's not just me—she's awkward too." But you have to feel strong enough to own the position.

I did a thirty-day experiment to test how personal professional stories compared to strictly knowledge-transfer stories on social media. Knowledge-transfer stories are the facts only or how-to articles, lists, or case studies that don't have a personal angle. I had far more engagement with personal professional stories that still had a business lens than with stories that were all business.

## ••• Bragging Right •••

When you've decided who you are and what you stand for, run everything through those filters instead of filtering yourself through the lenses of others. You already know you belong in the game, so gather your proof and put it on display so people can root for you.

**To Consider:** Are you a knowledge broker, an expert, or a visionary? (Refer to the definitions on page 155 for reference.)

**To Do:** Set up your professional story bank. As you think of a story from your life, add it to the file. It can be about anything. You don't have to write it out in full. Just jot down a few short sentences or words you know will jog your memory, say, about that time when you did or you saw something, or when something happened to you. If you hear someone tell a story you relate to, don't hesitate to include it and even reference them in your storytelling. Stories can be outrageous or simple and pure. Here's how simple a story bank can be:

**Story idea:** _____

**Keywords:** _____

**Point:** _____

**Synopsis:** _____

## Example

**Story idea:** *Young's Point: Go jump off a bridge*

**Keywords:** *beginner, fear, no fear, effort, left behind*

**Point**: *observer, a leap I won't make*

**Synopsis:** *Near my cottage at Stony Lake, Ontario, there's an old iron and steel truss bridge over water, and every summer children scale the trusses, climbing up, up, up to the highest point, then one, two, and jump into the rushing water below. Seeing them as they leap makes my stomach quiver. Even the smallest rarely hesitate when they're at the top. They're committed to the leap. I'm playing the role of the observer, seeing someone do a feat that I'm fascinated by but won't ever do.*

You can find a list of story bank prompts at: **LisaBragg.com.**

**To Share:** Ask people about a brag they have from this week. What's something that you can promote for them? Then do it.

# 11

# Know Who You Are

RIGHT AFTER my life in TV, I had to build networks and connections for my content business. I went to loads of networking events. I did speed networking, where the host says "go," and you run around the room collecting business cards. Don't do it. One time, after doing three meetings with one group, I actually refused to give someone a card. He already had three of my high-quality-stock cards. I didn't need another one of his cards, or his business—selling pens and squishy balls. If he couldn't remember me, then we weren't meant to do business. This racing around comes from the marketing funnel mindset: get as many contacts as you can and then email them about your product or service. Ugh. It so rarely works for people on either side, but it persists.

We need to adopt human-to-human relationships in an infinite loop, not to keep chasing people but to bring them into our world and nurture the relationships and see if we fit together. They may never be a client, but you might just put out the right piece of content that resonates with them. Maybe they tell someone else. Purposeful self-promotion isn't about funnels; it's about building relationships. The goal of networking is connections and, better yet, relationships. When we discover what connects us, we open ourselves up to be transformed by one another.

In your networking efforts, you want to pull people toward you. That's what happened when I started my own events for professionals and entrepreneurs. The only rule: no business cards. We gave each other knowledge and enjoyed each other's company as human beings. We became a community, and I had clients for a decade because of the relationships forged in it. Building communities is a huge way of expanding your repertoire of people you know. You need to reach out to people to move the elaborate conversations you imagine out into the world. You must let other people tap into your genius and also tap into theirs.

Trust is a currency of interactions, not transactions. It takes time to earn trust. You don't build it. By giving of yourself in a story, you signal trustworthiness. People get to know you, your values, your personality, your strengths. Trust forms over time with your connections; you initiate, develop, and then sustain the relationship. This is a long game. Earned trust is a precious asset.

## Affiliation

We went to the same school but decades apart, and that's enough to start a bond. We aren't related but share the same last name, and that's enough to make a bond. This is affiliation: "people like us do things like this." Creating an affiliation doesn't take much. It could be based on something as simple as having done something similar to someone else. If you can figure out what you have in common with someone, it makes it easier to build a bond. The question "What do I have in common with them?" moves you ahead in comfort with networking and connecting. If networking is scary for you, start by remembering that we're all humans.

## Cheerleaders, Mentors, Sponsors, and Champions

I'll commit to being your cheerleader. Cheerleaders can come from anywhere and everywhere. They're the people on the sidelines reminding you that you are valuable and they want you to keep going (or go further). Sharon Heck, chief tax officer at Intel and on the board of directors of the Intel Foundation, told me her cheerleaders have sometimes come from unexpected places. "My mentees are some of the biggest cheerleaders that I have," she said. "Now, as I've gotten older in my career, they're pushing me to say, 'Hey, we want to see somebody like you in leadership. You go get that for us.' It's been really cool." Don't just look ahead all the time; there's gold in current peers and those we lead or mentor.

Anyone can be a mentor, and anyone can be a mentee—age and stage don't matter; it's about sharing knowledge. We can learn from each other, once or over time. Mentoring others has fantastic benefits. (Remember to think of collaboration over competition.) Instead of trying to prove you're the smartest in the room, you'll be seen as the competent, generous one.

Sponsors are company trajectory gold. A sponsor advocates for you when you're not in the room. Sponsors are people with social currency or authority who are willing to use their power to help you. I'm often asked how to get a sponsor. It starts with being your own advocate, being seen and heard while also building relationships. There's no magic formula. You must commit to your networks and develop deeper connections. It takes time to cultivate a relationship that results in a person taking on this role for you. To get to this stage, you have to earn it—you must have social currency with them.

They bring you in because they want to tap into what you're thinking, saying, or doing. You've reached the stage at which other people promote you *for you*.

A champion is very much like a sponsor, except they're outside your current company or your industry. They can give you strategic input and are willing to use their social clout to help you win on a vaster scale. They'll be on the lookout for you, opening doors and recommending you for opportunities you haven't even dreamed are possible. You'll want to do the work in this book to make it easy for your potential champions to talk about you, to easily articulate your value and point to your social proof.

## Developing Reach

What follows are some key concepts to keep in mind about networking to help you develop reach. You should always market yourself to where you want to go.

Turn your network into connections that matter and are worthwhile. This is about quality, not quantity. Networking doesn't have to be self-serving if you go in feeling grateful and knowing that networking is a give-and-take exercise. If you feel as though you are offering instead of asking, you'll be more likely to participate. Take a leap of faith: it is uncomfortable to reach out to people you don't know, but people do it every day. Hit send. Ask for the meeting. What's the worst that could happen? Someone refuses your request. That's okay; just keep going. The more times you hear no, the closer you are to a yes.

### Network Anywhere

I live in Toronto, the fourth-largest North American city, and in the inner city. It's not a big deal for me to pop into an event. If you live far away from a city center and have to spend two hours commuting to get anywhere, you're not as likely to do it.

Nowadays, however, people are doing business and connecting from everywhere. Don't let geography be a barrier. You can meet people randomly who become great connections. I'm a member of online communities, and when people ask for help with something I'm an expert in, I'll offer to help. This has led to some wonderful relationships and collaborations. I hope we'll one day meet in person, but it's lovely to be connected in a meaningful way online. I've even done business after meeting people in airport waiting areas.

If you're in a big city center, it's critical to remember that there are awesome people in smaller regions who might just be that right-fit collaborator.

**Take It Slow**
Anna was listening to two incredible thinkers who owned a consultancy. She knew she had to work for them. At the end of the presentation, she approached them to say that she wanted to work for them. Even though they didn't have anything right then, she began developing a relationship with them. Now, more than ten years later, and four time zones away, Anna works with them regularly.

Look further ahead and consider whom you need as an ally in two years. It takes time to network, connect, and earn trust with people who are influential and can open more doors for you. Start sending signals in their direction today. When they finally see you, you're suddenly everywhere for them. If you have social proof they can discover in various places, they'll feel like they know you.

## Widen, Don't Winnow

Especially if you're experiencing a time of hardship, don't winnow your networks; widen them. We tend to want to go into ourselves, and talk only to the people immediately around us, but when we step into our wider network, we have more people who are likely to help. Don't go underground.

## Be a Connector

Develop a list of people you support, who you know are good, and share that list with others. You can ask people you meet if they want to be on your referral list. It helps build goodwill. Make introductions to others: one significant introduction can be life-changing.

## Trace Success

Get inspiration from other people, but don't copy what they're doing word for word, action for action. Success leaves clues. Who is three steps ahead of you? Who is one step ahead of you? Contact them and become collaborators. You don't have to reinvent; just make sure you're honoring who you are and not replicating other people. Successful people go off and do unique things, so their paths change. Their obligation is to their talent and to keep pushing it.

## Engage with Other People's Audiences

Comment on other people's posts. So few people do this. If you can think fast and have something of value to extend the conversation, that's great. But you can also copy a portion of their post and highlight what you liked about it. The original poster will become aware of you and so will those who see your comment.

## Use Connecting Techniques

Here are more tips to increase your reach:

- Go deep with the people you already know. Reconnect with them to make your relationships strong. Who is one degree away from you? That's a warm connection.

- Who haven't you talked to in three months? Do a quarterly follow-up.

- Who haven't you talked to in decades? Yes, the relationship went stale, but a friendly check-in is a nice touch.

- People seem a little too familiar? Get out of your silo. Having connections in different offices, sectors, regions, and nations is healthy. It helps keep your thinking diverse.

- Who do other people think you should know? Ask for warm introductions.

- Who do you just need to know? There are benefits to reaching out cold. If you have your social proof set up, the other person is more likely to see similarities. Don't ask for anything, but work to earn the relationship. If you want to develop and deepen a relationship, generate ideas for them.

- Get to know your client's clients, or the audience of the person you're looking to attract.

## ••• Bragging Right •••

Use all the bragging skills you've developed so far to give future you a big boost. Send your signal wide. You don't know who will make a difference in your life. We all need ego support. We all need people who help us feel like we matter—we need people to see and hear us. The more you can show others that you like and support them, the easier, the better.

**To Consider:** Are you actively building relationships to gain a sponsor or champion? You need these key people at every stage of your professional journey, and they do change with time.

**To Do:** You're being helped, so help someone else move forward. Always be a connector. Who can you introduce to each other? Make it a goal to connect two people each week. Both will remember you for bringing them together.

**To Share:** Tell a person about what it means to be a champion. Find out how they've championed others in the past (likely without the title of champion).

# 12

# Help People Talk about You

DEE DEE Taylor Eustace is a Toronto- and New York–based architect, interior designer, and developer. She has had repeat appearances on *Oprah*, been featured in loads of media, and has her own TV shows. For the past five years, Eustace took a break from actively self-promoting, but because she had built fantastic momentum, the awareness about her work and her achievements did not wane, and she kept getting opportunities. Now, she's back at it, having expanded her business to include a home goods curation company with her daughter, Rachel. It is as though she didn't miss a beat.

A client once called Eustace "plucky," and that's stuck with her. In our interview, she said she has experienced "stress and criticism and failure. You just keep going." As a woman working internationally, she found she often had to set the record straight about her experience, expertise, and success. When she owned a construction and millwork company, she needed to, as she put it, "pull out her credentials cards" to be taken seriously. She said, "What other people don't realize is that you have to speak their language."

You might aspire to reach Eustace's level, to be recognized and promoted by your clients and peers at a North American level (that's wide-field and off-field), or you might want something more local, within your organization or with a smaller group. But whatever level you are working toward, the idea is the same. Your positioning helps get you more opportunities and eventually enough that you don't have to continually raise your hand. People who don't know you personally endorse you. They've heard of you. They want you. They don't bring you in necessarily because you know X, Y, and Z—they bring you in because they want to tap into what you're thinking, saying, or doing. You've reached the stage at which other people promote you *for you*.

To achieve this, you need to think strategically and make it easy for others to speak about you. Think of your small wins building over time, gaining momentum so that it seems the opportunities and growth just come on their own. Like a flywheel, you've removed the friction from gaining opportunities so you now have traction. You will need to put enough content online on public or internal platforms so that people who are once or twice removed can look you up and see that you have what they need. You need to give people something memorable about you so they can say, "Oh, yes, talk to her. She's the one you need." This means, at the foundational level, filling out the forms for the associations you belong to and having an up-to-date profile that's visible online (such as your own website, or use a social media platform) so you show up when people search for you. Then you can produce things like articles, podcasts, and videos to put out into the world. When people search for your topic, they find out about you.

At the next level, it's others showcasing you. It's you in a newsletter, on a panel, giving a keynote, and gaining media coverage. You'll reach new audiences; they'll then search for you, find out more about you, and more opportunities will come.

## From Passive Audience to Brand Ambassador

You may already have brand ambassadors, which is terrific. A brand ambassador is someone who recommends you even if they don't really know you. They like what you do and are bragging about you. These are wonderful human beings.

Once you are putting content out into the world regularly, you'll start to have a passive audience who follows you. In social media parlance, they're called "lurkers." They are in the background enjoying what you're doing, slowly becoming brand ambassadors. Lurkers might not be commenting on or liking your posts. Many people simply don't think that is important to do—do you comment and like every post? They might not even be in your realm, but given the opportunity, they may want to engage with you or refer you to someone else. As you build success, a lot is happening in the background that you aren't aware of. When you have your flywheel going, success may come to you at odd times.

Let's go back to Neela White, the wealth advisor and aging specialist I mentioned earlier. After taking care of her elderly parents for almost a decade, she wanted to change the conversation around elder care so that there was more honesty about financial needs in later life. She found that by the time people had the conversation, it was often too late to do any significant financial planning. Most of us think we'll be healthy until we're ninety-five and then drop dead. White's posts would convince you otherwise, but she wasn't getting a lot of traction with them.

From time to time, White thought she might give up, that her posts were not making an impact, but one day, Chris, a loose connection on a social media channel, introduced her to a person who became a client. White didn't know Chris, but he told her he had been watching her posts and thought she would be the best to help his client. He wanted to be a connector, and he already knew from her posts that White was the right fit for his client's needs. So she discovered that what she was doing was working. She has high social currency now. One thing does lead to another—it's just not a straight path.

Here's a caveat, though: when you're an expert, like White, people in your industry, too, follow you; some will copy your work, and others who want something for nothing are ready to pounce. While I'm all for "give, give, give," eventually there has to be "a take" on your part. Think of posting as an investment. Used judiciously, your knowledge has value that will translate into business, visibility, or opportunities.

You can be seen and heard just by putting your ideas out there in a way that is convenient for others to access. The media goes to the same people repeatedly because they are convenient. Make sure you are easy to find, but avoid the temptation to buy an audience. Some people purchase "ghost followers" to get a book deal, for vanity metrics, or just because (surprisingly) it isn't expensive. But the followers you buy don't care about you or the message you want to send; they're not making any personal recommendations. Fake followers just follow, post, and repost the clients who have purchased them. Removing them takes quite a bit of work. In 2018, the *New York Times* did an excellent exposé on fake followers and their effect. As celebrities, athletes, politicians, and more have many fake followers, the prevailing attitude seems to be "Well, everyone is doing it," but as the article also explained, "popularity has a price." Purchased followers can be tracked, exposing the person who bought followers and thus throwing their credibility into question. In addition, many of the purchased followers are automated fake accounts, and large-scale social identity theft has become a major issue. Buying the appearance of greater influence carries too great of a risk to your credibility.

Think strategically and make it easy for others to speak about you.

## Hiring Assistance

Do the work in this book first before hiring additional help. You want to know your intention and what makes you remarkable before you ask someone to write or amplify your messages. If you skip the hard work of strategy to go right to tactics (for example, videos, podcasts, social media), you'll throw away your money.

Loads of people do get help, by the way—you just don't necessarily see it. I met Maria at a conference. As former journalists, we had a lot in common. I asked her why she was attending the conference. She said it wasn't about the conference at all. She was building the profile of Veronica, a VP of the British region of an international firm. Maria was hired not by the firm but by Veronica directly to do publicity and public relations to build up her industry profile (wide-field visibility). Maria's job was to follow Veronica, develop stories around her interactions, and then write articles for association magazines and pitch media outlets. She took pictures of Veronica during a panel she spoke on and with many of the high-profile industry speakers for social posts. I suggested that Maria help Veronica send every key person she met a quick personal note and a photo too.

Veronica was moving up quickly in her company, but she wanted a faster boost. She is now the regional CEO of her company. Having the additional profile, I'm sure, helped her to get where she was going faster.

## Media Coverage

Remember Joe Foster, from Reebok, whom I mentioned in chapter 9? His grandfather was also huge in the shoe industry. We can learn something from "Grandad Joe." He pioneered the spiked running shoe, but his genius wasn't just in making that product: he was excellent at marketing it. He used influencers of the day to champion his running shoes, giving shoes away to reporters so they would write articles about them (which they did) and to athletes to run in them. "Grandad Joe" had an awesome product the world wanted, but he knew he also needed the product to be seen, accepted, and recognized in order to have success. The Joe Foster of our time noted, "Genius doesn't just rely on creativity, invention, and production. It also needs recognition. Without being recognized, you can't be perceived as a genius."

If you're looking for media coverage, know that it takes a lot of work and must be in service of someone else. So many people think being in the media will translate into automatic sales, but it doesn't. It adds to your profile. It might drive a small percentage of people to your social channels or other platforms. They might want to know what else you're thinking after you were so generous in your clip. It's one touch among the many that you'll have. You need many touchpoints, such as your personal website, a free gift of knowledge that they can take off your site (a lead magnet, an ebook), articles, videos, podcasts, or a newsletter. I know so many people who think, *If I just get on the number one show in the nation, it will change everything.* Nope. You must show up again and again and again. It is a long game.

Be ready and willing to say yes if the media does call. If you simply can't do an interview, be ready to suggest someone else who is fantastic but who rarely gets the opportunity. The media and the person you recommend will thank you and remember you because you are a connector willing to help.

Podcast episodes and streaming shows are also effective ways to share your work with the world. You can host your own show or be a guest on someone else's. The advantage of being on someone else's show is that a different audience from your own will become aware of you. If you are a guest, be a good one. That means promoting the show to your friends, family, and coworkers. The host also wants to reach new audiences. When I have a guest on my podcast, I'll often look through my social channels to see whom we have in common, and then send our mutual acquaintance a direct message about the episode. It's a lovely way to reconnect and bring value to others. It's a soft way of saying, "Hey, look, I made this thing," which is bragging. While you may want to profile others on your show, people need to hear your thoughts, so do a solo show from time to time. Be sure to amplify it. So many people fail to market their show, and then they're surprised that no one watches or listens to it.

If you want some extra buzz around a particular event or product, you'll need to have your intention, audience, and credibility already set up. Then you can promote in a range of areas so that you appear everywhere. At the buzz stage, consider bringing in PR experts to take care of the promotion blast while you do the good work you're supposed to be doing.

## Pep Talks

Time for a bit of a pep talk. I am proud of you. See what I'm doing there? Do you give yourself pep talks? If no one else is going to do it for you, you need to do it for yourself. Even if everyone is encouraging you, you need to be your biggest hype person. Post a sticky note on your computer with your new title: Chief Hype Officer. Get excited about what you're doing. You have lots of shots at opportunity. Keep motivated. It's an ongoing journey, so keep cheering for yourself.

## ••• Bragging Right •••

Other people need to see and hear you before they'll brag for you! And when they do, they'll be the promotion machine that propels you even further, and with much less effort. If you're given a profile, embrace it. People are looking for you to show them the way. Own the social currency you've earned with grace.

**To Consider:** Who has already come to you from a connection generated indirectly by your bragging? How did they find you?

**To Do:** Research podcasts or other shows you want to be on. Look for ones where people you admire and who work in the same field as you have already been featured as guests. Listen to some of the episodes. This "follow along" strategy is often used by people looking for opportunities in speaking and in media.

If you were a guest, what would you talk about? What three critical points would you want to convey? What would you want the audience to do at the end of your talk?

Research how to become a guest on the show and take the steps. This usually involves writing to the host or producer. Don't be discouraged if you have to follow up. The top shows have many requests.

**To Share:** Share Joe Foster's quote: "Genius doesn't just rely on creativity, invention, and production. It also needs recognition. Without being recognized, you can't be perceived as a genius." Either email it to five friends or post it on social media and tag five friends who are brilliant and just need some more recognition.

… **13**

# Lead Others to Shine

HELPING OTHERS brag is an imperative part of being a leader. As I've said before, people want to be seen and heard. A culture that recognizes valuable contributions connects people to their work in a more meaningful way. Helping people be proactive and own their achievements, along with setting a team environment that is bragworthy, is a catalyst for future success. What helps your people will help you as their leader. The company will look more attractive to others, including potential employees, stakeholders, and clients. This is what's known as the "halo effect," specifically "the tendency for positive impressions of a person, company, brand, or product in one area to positively influence one's opinion or feelings in other areas." As a leader, you'll help the talent pipeline by encouraging people to learn these skills so that in the future, they'll be able to self-identify for opportunities. If you're a mentor, sponsor, or coach, you'll want to learn how to best help others brag and self-promote. It also helps you shine a light on the accomplishments that matter to those you serve.

People don't want to work somewhere stale. They want a company that is looking out for them personally and professionally. For some, recognition is as valuable as money, vacation time, or titles. When people know their value and are able to share it, they feel psychologically safer too. Foster an environment that encourages acknowledgment and a celebration of wisdom, and consider systems that help everyone flourish (and watch for those that don't).

Bragging right means helping everyone rise. You don't need to be the loudest or always the most visible. You might be worried that you'll not be seen within your organization if you pass the mic, but there are many ways to be seen. Don't feel threatened if someone increases their visibility. You can make room on the stage for one more voice.

Mita Mallick used to play small. In an interview, she told me how she used to hide at the back of the room, sitting on the radiator. Hearing she would never make it to the director level was her wake-up call. Now Mallick is a head of inclusion, equity, and impact in corporate America. She's amassed a huge following because of her posts on diversity and inclusion. She's also the co-host of *The Brown Table Talk* podcast with Dee C. Marshall.

"Culturally, I was raised with the ethos 'children are to be seen, not to be heard,'" she told me. "Never call anyone by their first name, never question authority, always defer to authority. And then all of a sudden, I show up in corporate America, and I was trying to unlearn all this stuff. And there's a big piece of being hospitable, welcoming, never making anyone feel uncomfortable, and being humble. I realized that humility has been a disservice to me in my career in corporate. I have a vision board with the words 'Stay humble. Hustle hard. Be kind.' So, I subscribe to that, but I culturally need to watch the humility piece. Earlier in my career, I didn't brag, didn't talk about money, didn't talk about what I accomplished." But that approach failed her.

Mallick continued: "I tell my team, I never used to keep track of all my wins at work. But if I don't remember them, who else is going to remember them? The fairy godmother who's late and never showed up to promote me? So now I tell my team, or anyone I'm coaching, whether it's in an Excel spreadsheet or a Google doc, document your wins each month."

Collectively we forget wins so easily because we're on to the next goal or emergency. We're humans and can't keep track of it all. Helping your team log their braggable moments will ultimately be a gift to you too. You're human and can't remember everything they've worked on. Set them up to do a self-review in advance of their talent review. Have them share a quick list with you when you meet to talk about progress. You'll likely hear about "invisible accomplishments" and see significant moments of learning and growth. Give the people you lead clues for the signals of success, which include personal greatness, engaging greatness in others, and business acumen (so often people forget to share that they understand the business strategy). They'll feel much more seen and heard. Be sure it isn't just a box they check or numbers in a grid.

The very common old-school phrase in business "the results speak for themselves" is a guardian of the status quo—it's how things stay the same. Guide them to realize that the next level is attaching meaning to the results. Also, have them think about the results from the listener's perspective. The listener simply doesn't know all you know. That's why you have to talk about your work with purpose.

Only praising and considering results sets up a culture and communication style that makes our work relationships transactional. As a leader, you want to build beyond that transactional feeling to have people feel safe and part of the community (connected, informed, and engaged)—especially if you have team members who work remotely. This chapter helps with increasing the "social glue" that bonds your team members with you, each other, and the business.

• • •

# Bragging right means helping everyone rise.

• • •

## Great and Grateful

Sometimes, people need tools to know how to brag about themselves. Leadership coach Emily Feairs and I have the same type of clients—ambitious leaders and world changers—and many struggle to come up with their weekly brags. They can tell you what went wrong, but what went well is much, much harder to talk about.

Feairs decided to help her young children think about owning their wins differently in a family practice they do every day called "Great and Grateful." Her children do it by saying statements like "I'm grateful for the sunshine, and I'm great because I talked to Michelle, who was all alone at recess." Most of your people probably know how to express gratitude, but if they don't talk about how they are great, too, they are abdicating responsibility for themselves. In an interview with me, Feairs said, "We have a responsibility to lean into our greatness, to own it, to take responsibility for showing up and the full Technicolor version of our greatness. Otherwise, we're cutting short the impact on the world that we want to have. I'm going to show up in the full way that I can. It's an ecosystem of needing both those things."

When you're coaching your team, help them balance their failures with their success stories. Bragging is an upward spiral of momentum. In many leadership and personal success books, the idea is to talk about failures, but first your people need to understand and own their successes. Your workplace will be a safer place when your team is not just looking for what's going wrong but also looking for what's going right.

One reason people are burning out is that they feel no one sees or hears them and that their work doesn't matter. By leaning into listening and looking for success, you help them feel connected more deeply to their work because they feel assured that what they do matters to someone. When a culture celebrates the successes of all its members, it gives a stronger sense of belonging to all its members. This isn't about everyone getting a trophy for just showing up. It's about acknowledging and celebrating that everyone has a valuable contribution and deserves to be seen and heard.

There are all kinds of tools in this book that you can offer your team members, or the individual contributors you take care of, to support them on their own quest to brag. But remember, everyone isn't like you. People do take cues from you, though. If you have loads of confidence, are highly charismatic, and expect your team to self-nominate, know that some of your team might struggle with it. You set the stage, so encourage those who might be sitting at the back of the room to have one-on-one time to tell you their brags.

Keep a lookout for those who overprepare or have perfectionist tendencies. They likely have a load of brags filling up their brag book that they're ready to tell you, but they might be waiting to be asked or waiting for the right time. Make it the right time by creating an intentional and safe culture of bragging. Consider how you can track and acknowledge contributions instead of always putting it on your employees to share their successes. Everyone needs an intentional file that holds their own kudos and nods—yes, a brag book. Ask people to share a few items from the past as you start sharing on a regular schedule. Have your team think of their personal greatness, how they engage greatness in others, and their business acumen as bragging rights.

Are you aware of the message over the messenger? Just as I use my magic wand to bestow expert status on my clients, you have that ability too. You can do it proactively. Brag for your new team members in advance. Consider Vivian Pickard's advice

I shared earlier to always walk into a room "as a ten." In this sense, you are critical to scaffolding your team members' success. You can give informal authority and credibility for them to be known and seen widely as people with something to contribute by signaling their value before they join the call or walk in the door. Giving someone credibility means they don't have to seek it from others. They can move right into contribution mode without distraction.

## Self-Deprecating Humor

As a person in power, you might have mastered the art of self-deprecating humor as a bridge to others, and you might be able to afford a laugh at your own expense. But self-deprecation often backfires because people don't always get the nuances, and it doesn't always work very well cross-culturally. It can widen the divide. (See chapter 7 for the quote by Hannah Gadsby.) If you have self-deprecating team members, you may not be able to hear and see their achievements easily. Listen for their signals of "it's nothing," or other deflection, and make a mental note of it and follow up. Look beyond what they're reporting. Approach the person with thoughtfulness and curiosity.

Self-deprecation is an ingrained response for some people. It's armor that's part of self, self-worth, and identity. You might have employees who take their self-deprecation to deeper levels with "I always screw everything up!" or other disparaging remarks. That's going to need some deeper consideration and coaching. It's important for the person to see that no one is perfect. You can give someone a starter script as a coaching point. Suggest that when they receive a compliment, they say, "I'm so glad I could help." Bragging and self-promotion activities help support psychological safety because they foster self-awareness and create a sense of belonging, recognition, and culture. These activities also help increase a workplace that includes active listening and feedback.

## Supporting a Team That Brags

When you're starting this employee engagement strategy, set your team up for some quick wins. Remember to celebrate moments and not just milestones. You can also set up your team for a win that you'll celebrate next quarter. Consider what the brag looks and feels like. Start to plan it now.

I mentioned Rita and Eleanor in chapter 3 in a story about meritocracy: Rita had spent all her time making her boss look good and had neglected to self-promote—she had expected her work to speak for itself and that her boss would help her climb the ranks. But that did not happen, and now she was doing the same thing at her new job. But Eleanor, Rita's VP, was not and did not want to be responsible for Rita's success; Rita needed to learn to build her own career through self-promotion while helping others. I was brought in to help them with team cohesion and engagement. One exercise we did was to create a group brag goal: they would be the most (positively) well-known team in the firm. The partners would understand how they were a team of rock stars. Not only did this help them work on their individual goals to be seen and heard, but also doing it collectively made it easy and fun (collaboration over competition). Less than a year later, in a follow-up session, they shared their stories of glory. They had been individually and collectively featured in newsletters and panels. They also had lovely emails and positive performance reviews from the partners.

For individuals, talking about success is a combination of knowing and trusting one's own greatness but also remaining grounded. It's not just about how awesome a person is but also about their knowing that other people have supported them along the way, and that opportunities arose through timing and tenacity. You can coach all your team members, those who brag easily and those who struggle with it, to talk about their brags using these bigger-picture prompts. Ask them:

- Who mentored you?
- Who sponsored you?
- Who was a champion who used their social capital to get you here?
- Who took a risk on you?
- Who gave you an opportunity?
- What did you learn?
- What can you teach from this experience?
- Who else on your team contributed?
- Who else is doing a good job?
- How did luck contribute to your success?
- Have you displayed gratitude?
- In what ways can you show appreciation?

You can also use four guiding principles to help everyone on your team stay grounded in their bragging and look good while doing it. I call this the "Others Technique":

- Promote others
- Introduce others
- Help others
- Let others say good things about you

## Co-promote

Think back to "sistering up" or "shine theory," and set a goal of co-promotion with your team: when they talk about themselves, they also have to have a brag ready that includes someone else. This co-promotion strategy helps perpetuate a spirit of collaboration, and the outcome will build connections and trust. It also helps those involved in the co-promotion strategy to understand their roles and how others desire credit. You'll hear less squabbling about who should take credit for what performance aspect and be able to ask more questions about the achievements of team members. Ask them, as part of any team project, to think about what they want to co-promote each other for, so they can negotiate credit without you being involved. In a team meeting, discuss co-promotion, why you do it, and how it works in action on your team. What's the Goldilocks zone for your environment—where it feels just right? What does co-promotion sound like, look like, and, if it helps, what is the opposite that could be detrimental?

Self-promotion in an office is all about context. As the leader, overall you set the zone and tone of co-promotion. You need to model what it looks like in the environment. If your office is full of self-promoters, you'll really need to be on the lookout for those who don't promote. Just like Eleanor in Rita's story, you don't want to be responsible for anyone's professional journey—your job is to support.

Keep in mind, as well, that when you host team social events, not everyone can come out to schmooze with you. Caregiving responsibilities limit people's ability to attend many after-hours social events. Don't only brag about the people who are most social. Hold your team members to this rule as well.

"Her victory is your victory. Celebrate with her. Your victory is her victory. Point to her."

ABBY WAMBACH

The idea that "team players don't take credit" is a myth. Researchers have found that we tend to want to reward only one person for work. Researchers at Cornell University and Ohio State University found that team winning streaks don't change our ideas of what we think humans can achieve as much as "streaking stars"—individuals who give impressive performances. Think Usain Bolt winning three gold medals in a row. Something about seeing a single person succeed lights us up. We want to witness those who have skill, talent, and ingenuity. The researchers found this was true in organizations, too, which is why we're seeing more and more celebrity CEOs and star employees. We enjoy being inspired and being in awe of others, and we want that joy to continue.

On the flip side, though, many companies are trying to move stories away from the CEO or powerful employees and instead toward the company brand. Moving away from the "hero leader myth" makes sense in some cases. Part of the reason for this approach is that companies are fearful of missteps by the humans that make up the company. They're also concerned that they're building brands for people who then leave and take their effort to other companies. While limiting CEO hero stories is fine, limiting the stories of your team members is shaky ground.

Humans want stories of humans. People care about people. People follow people, more so than they follow brands. If you're a leader telling your staff that they should only promote the company, you're taking a large risk. I've consulted with teams on how to "allow" and help team members tell success stories on their personal and professional channels, even if it is a company with sensitive and confidential information. If you deny or frown upon people telling their stories, you deny the social capital that self-promotion gives your team members. That's quite valuable for them for now, and it is security for their futures.

If you're really pushing the one big brand story and doing less employee-based storytelling, you'll need to watch that your teams don't feel like their identities are being scratched away for one behemoth brand. My recommendation is to tell more stories, not less. Everyone needs to see themselves in the stories, in a way that connects to the head, heart, and gut.

## The Road to a Promotion

How clear is the path to promotion on your team or in your organization? If you're HR, you're likely saying, "Crystal clear." But respondents to the Bragging Rights research question "How do people get a promotion in your work environment?" said that there are "fuzzy unwritten rules" that trump everything else, or that "leadership chooses," which isn't a clear path. Only a small group said, "We have systems in place to nominate people." In the survey, many people commented that they had left corporate to become self-employed because the road to the next level had been blocked and unclear. About a quarter said they had to self-advocate. Leaders often want to give themselves wiggle room, but when rules are unclear, it makes people distrustful. With rules you can live with, you'll help earn more social capital within your team.

Take a situation at Google as a cautionary tale. Women weren't moving ahead and Google couldn't figure out why. In 2012, the tech company looked at its hiring data and saw that many women weren't getting past the initial phone interview, and if they did, then they weren't getting promoted at the same rate as men. What the company realized was that their hiring practices included listening for people to talk about their accomplishments, and they were used to men flaunting their achievements. When women didn't, they thought they were unaccomplished. They've since added women to the hiring process to listen for the more subtle bragging cues women give.

Like a growing number of companies, Google also uses a self-selection process: you can nominate yourself for a promotion. You also need to actively solicit endorsements about your work from colleagues. Women tend to feel less comfortable self-advocating than men, so fewer women were participating. Internally, the company began doing workshops to close the gap. Google employee Anna Vainer founded a workshop to help participants specifically feel more comfortable self-promoting. Focused on encouraging people to speak openly about accomplishments in the workplace and beyond, Google's #IAmRemarkable is now offered worldwide as a program to foster diversity and allyship. The program challenges participants to think about how they are remarkable and to consider how we listen to each other in the workplace.

Interestingly, we tend to assume men know what they're talking about unless they prove otherwise, and that women don't know what they're talking about until they prove they do. So constantly check your assumptions, and encourage everyone, no matter who they are, to show proof of their brags. Simple invitations like "Tell me more about that" or "Tell me more about your role" and questions such as "What did other people do?" can unpack a lot. Assumptions are the reason we have charismatic leadership without the required substance and competence.

Starting a company-wide bragging rights community of practice to help your thought leaders and social connectors, along with those who want to be on the path, gives your company incredible benefits. It helps connect more members of your team who are at different levels, fosters conversations around gender bias in the workplace, and shows that you care about the personal-professional journey of your teams.

This is what we can call "bragitude." (The alternative was "antigloat," but people liked "bragitude" better.) No, I didn't make it up. It's an intervention designed by researchers to increase *freudenfreude* (which means the lovely enjoyment of another person's success, as mentioned in chapter 6). Bragitude (short for "brag plus gratitude") is intentionally tying words of gratitude to the listener following discussions of personal successes. In other words, share your win, then tell the person how they helped you accomplish it. For example, "I'm getting a promotion, thanks to your tips on how to navigate the new process" or "Thank you for being there. I couldn't have done this without you," along with your clear brag.

Another term from the same research is "shoy," which means "intentionally sharing the joy of someone relating a success story by showing interest and asking follow-up questions."

In this research study, the college students who initially had mild depression and began to practice bragitude and shoy reported that the feeling of *freudenfreude* came easier after two weeks, along with enhanced relationships, improved moods, and greater generosity. It also helped emphasize compassionate caring and lessened unhealthy competitive striving.

Here's how to help develop shoy and bragitude among you and your team (hint: it starts with active listening):

1  Increase your expressions of shared joy when others report a success or positive experience.

2  Increase sharing the credit when you report your own successes to others.

3  Increase your nurturance of others.

### ••• Bragging Right •••

Helping people shine could make you the best leader ever. The one they'll remember. Creating space for people to talk about their work successes, to be seen and be heard, is invaluable to the team and the organization.

**To Consider (a):** Are you helping only those who are great at schmoozing with you? Are you sure?

**To Consider (b):** In your organization, what obstacles need to be removed so that self-promotion and bragging are acceptable and encouraged?

**To Do (a):** What's your Great and Grateful for today? List at least two things that made you great and two things that you are grateful for today. Bonus points if you do this with someone else.

**To Do (b):** Help your team help you to be the best leader. (You'll be able to brag about how successful your team is.) Prompt them to do this exercise:

Write down and be ready to have a conversation with me about your answers to two prompts:

1. Here's what I would like for my career.
2. Here's how you can help.

Then they have this concrete ask: "Would you be willing to do that?" So often, we tell people what we want for our future, but we don't ask for anything, so people don't know how to help us—hence the importance of the concrete ask. Now, you don't have to be able or willing to do it, but doing something is necessary. You can suggest that they reach out to a broader network to help with other components.

**To Share:** Share the Others Technique on page 197 with your peers and team.

# 14

# No Longer a Hidden Gem

IN THE Bragging Rights research survey, 70 percent of respondents agreed with the statement "I have been too humble at times and it has cost me opportunities." People who reflected on their professional journeys and saw missed opportunities wrote, "In the past, I missed out on winning projects because I failed to highlight my powerful successes," "I didn't get promoted after my mat leave because I wasn't able to articulate my value," "I wrongly assumed my manager was sharing my accomplishments with executive leadership," and "I have been very patient in waiting for recognition, always proving myself first. As a result, salary increases and promotions took years longer for me than for others. Ultimately the result is fewer years as a high earner before retirement. The impact could be 7 figures." If you're tempted to give up or keep quiet about yourself, think of these people. There were more than 165 written responses, and many of them detailed at length their regret for not bragging.

Some people have been self-promoting for a long time. They might also be dedicated to doing it while they're not working. They might have been given a big profile by a company they worked for, or just got lucky with the timing of how a social network came online when they were there (right place, right time).

There's often luck and privilege that goes along with audience building and self-promotion landing in the strongest ways. For anything to really land, it is a long game. Even if you want buzz for only one thing, you should already have a solid foundation.

As bragging starts to work for you, don't stop at the first sign of challenge or success. Don't get caught in the need for validation, likes, or the illusory boon of success. Jeffrey Shaw, whom you met in chapter 4, told me in a chat, "Recognition isn't a destination." You can have twenty thousand followers, likes, and comments, but they are not a measure of your worth. Don't tie your self-worth to outcomes, because some of this work is outside your control. External validation, results, recognition, rewards—you can get sucked into a cycle of striving that hurts your well-being. If you come back to the idea that this is about showing up to make a meaningful contribution, the joy will come from within.

## The New Perfect Is 75 Percent

Lorne Michaels, the executive producer of *Saturday Night Live*, said, "The show doesn't go on because it's ready; it goes on because it's 11:30." You'll never be ready if you're waiting for "ready." Set a deadline and go, even if you aren't ready. Actor and writer Tina Fey adds to Michaels's quote in her book, *Bossypants*:

> You have to try your hardest to be at the top of your game and improve every joke you can until the last possible second, and then you have to let it go. You can't be that kid standing at the top of the waterslide, overthinking it. You have to go down the chute. (And I'm from a generation where a lot of people died on waterslides, so this was an important lesson for me to learn.) You have to let people see what you wrote. It will never be perfect, but perfect is overrated. Perfect is boring on live TV.

What I learned about "bombing" as an improviser at Second City was that bombing is painful, but it doesn't kill you. No matter how badly an improv set goes, you will still be physically alive when it's over. What I learned about bombing as a writer at *Saturday Night* is that you can't be too worried about your "permanent record." Yes, you're going to write some sketches that you love and are proud of forever—your golden nuggets. But you're also going to write some real shit nuggets. And unfortunately, sometimes the shit nuggets will make it onto the air. You can't worry about it. As long as you know the difference, you can go back to panning for gold on Monday.

Your audiences need to hear and see your thinking. Showing that your work is evolving, thinking out loud, failing, and being imperfect is hard for many of us to do. We hide our work until it is perfect, but in the meantime, we lose out on opportunities to make it better together—and we hide our impact and contribution. Good enough is good enough. Your imperfect presence is needed. You just have to be a plausible, comfortable version of yourself. Count it brag-worthy at 75 percent and know other people are doing it at a lot less. Throw out comedian Steve Martin's idea of being "so good they can't ignore you." It just keeps you working harder and waiting. Be great already and tell everyone.

## The Potential Factor

Potential, not simply your reputation, is critical to your future. John told two people about a job with an international firm in France. He thought Zara and Tom would both be a good fit; they had good reputations and loads of promise. Zara looked at the job and disqualified herself. She didn't have all the criteria. Tom

• • •

Potential, not simply your reputation, is critical to your future.

• • •

looked at the job and believed he could make it work; he knew he could figure it out. Zara also dismissed herself from applying because the job was in France. Tom didn't want to move, either, but he still applied. Tom got the job. They hired him based on the potential he showed. No one in the world had even 50 percent of the criteria and qualifications listed. Tom didn't move to France, either. It wasn't a determining factor: the HR team had included it, but the C-suite was open to negotiating. Believe you can be judged on potential, on promise, and not solely on your past or present.

As reported in a 2022 article by Matthew Easterbrook, social psychologists have found that doing a value affirmation exercise can have transformative power before stressful situations such as tests, presentations, or putting yourself out into the world, particularly if you feel stereotyped (by social or economic status, for example). Affirming your values helps restore your sense of equilibrium. Several studies, Easterbrook says, have found that the exercise also helps the feeling of authenticity and perceived authenticity (that is, it helps your communication skills when you've thought about your values).

What is central to your life? Choose two or three values that are most important to you. Focus on your thoughts and feelings. Then write about them for ten minutes. Easterbrook says that connecting to your values "can broaden your horizons, widen your attention, extend the cognitive resources you can draw on."

## There's No Stopping You, But...

Here's what could stop you: stopping. You might take a small time-out and then not feel like getting back to it.

Don't let technology stop you.

Don't let the naysayers stop you.

Don't let shame stop you.

Don't let your parents stop you. (Even the whisper of their thoughts. They didn't know how important talking about yourself would be to your career.)

Don't let your partner stop you.

Don't let your age stop you. You can brag and self-promote at any age. Don't wait until you reach a certain age.

Don't ask everyone for critique. You get that in your own head all the time.

Don't wait for likes or engagement. People *are* watching and listening; you just may not know it until they connect you to a client or write you a note thanking you years later.

Don't let the noise get to you.

Don't let the fear of being irrelevant and invisible hold you back.

Don't go for another certificate. If you do, make sure you're putting out your knowledge as you go.

Don't minimize what you do. It's so easy to say, "It was nothing." Celebrate successes, even small ones.

Don't wait for the end.

Find community.

Find compassion for yourself.

Find time, or, more realistically, allow energy for this work.

Share your value with the world. We need you in any way you want to share.

If you're taking a break from the world of work, make bragging and self-promotion your side project.

If you're returning to the world of work—ever—make bragging and self-promotion your side project.

Mistakes to be on the lookout for include self-sabotage, devaluing your worth, and procrastinating.

When you feel uncomfortable with bragging and self-promotion, open your brain a little more. A course on influence at Yale University suggests a magic question that can turn into the road map for your future, and it positively works: when you get a no or feedback that isn't helpful, ask, "What will it take?" I suggest priming your brain to come up with solutions for yourself to move forward using the same question. What will it take?

## The Spotlight Effect

"Last month I didn't do [fill in the blank] tactic to amplify my success." It could be social media, your newsletter, blog, video—whatever it is, don't worry. While it's important to have consistency, people likely aren't watching that closely.

The same goes with putting out the same content on repeat. People believe they're being noticed more than they really are. It's called the Spotlight Effect. We're the center of our own world, so we're watching all the time; the rest of the world, however, isn't. Put yourself in the perspective of your audience. How closely are you watching anyone else? That's why celebrities and politicians go out with the same talking points and repeat them often. A fan did a "supercut" montage of Lady Gaga's media tour for the movie *A Star Is Born* during which she repeats a phrase at least ten times with little variation: "There can be a hundred people in the room and ninety-nine don't believe in you, but just one does and it changes your whole life." She said it with conviction every time, as if each time was the only time. She didn't change her message, only her audience (except for the superfans who follow her around everywhere!).

The lovely people at a corner store I stop at on my way out of town always remember me. I go in there usually only when picking up a pizza at the joint next door, but we always chat. The last time I was in, they said, "Hey, caught you on the news awhile ago." I hadn't been at the TV station in two years. When you are consistent over longer periods, if you take a break, people think *they* missed seeing you, *they* missed something. So if you miss a month of posting on social media or sending your newsletter, don't fret. Just get back to doing it.

It's the same thing if you make a mistake during a presentation, speech, or conversation. People likely didn't notice, but if they did, they probably didn't think too much of it anyway (so no need to crawl into a hole).

## Hit Repeat

I'm going to repeat this: repeat yourself. People need continued exposure to an idea for it to stick. In leadership or speech training, the advice is frequently to tell your audience what you're going to tell them, then tell them, and then tell them what you just told them. It's okay to repeat a social media post, for example, so give yourself permission to have several on rotation. If you have only three pillars, the messages will be focused and, when repeated, effective.

"Healthy striving is self-focused: 'How can I improve?' Perfectionism is other-focused: 'What will they think?'"

BRENÉ BROWN

## Breathe

Becky Hemsley hadn't intended to so widely share a poem she'd written, but it became a viral sensation when she did post it. When I stumbled across the poem, called "Breathe," the author credit was "Anonymous." A quick search led me to Hemsley, and I asked her why she had wanted to be unknown. "There is an element of imposter syndrome sometimes," she said, "because I always thought [the poem] was so simple. I read other poems, and I think, *Gosh, how is this anything near that?* It's just supposed to make you feel something. So, if it makes people feel something, then that's the most important thing."

Initially, she had relegated the poem to her personal journal forever. "The only reason I ended up sharing it was because I met with a friend for coffee, and she was telling me how she was having a bit of a rough time at work. She said to me, 'I just feel like I can't win at all. You know, I feel like nothing I do is good enough. But then when I do something good, I play it down.' That's why I shared it. Then it kind of blew up. Everyone was saying that it really resonated with them."

With her success, Hemsley has left her teaching career to write and publish more poetry. She has graciously permitted me to share "Breathe" with you here.

## Breathe

she sat at the back
and they said she was shy
she led from the front
and they hated her pride

they asked her advice
and then questioned her guidance
they branded her loud
then were shocked by her silence

when she shared no ambition
they said it was sad
so she told them her dreams
and they said she was mad

they told her they'd listen
then covered their ears
and gave her a hug
whilst they laughed at her fears

and she listened to all of it
thinking she should,
be the girl they told her to be
best as she could

but one day she asked
what was best for herself
instead of trying
to please everyone else

so she walked to the forest
and stood with the trees
she heard the wind whisper
and dance with the leaves

And she spoke to the willow,
the elm and the pine
and she told them what she'd
    been told
time after time

she told them she never
felt nearly enough
she was either too little
or far, far too much

too loud or too quiet
too fierce or too weak
too wise or too foolish
too bold or too meek

then she found a small clearing
surrounded by firs
and she stopped and she heard
what the trees said to her

and she sat there for hours
not wanting to leave
for the forest said nothing . . .
it just let her breathe.

### ••• Bragging Right •••

Be kind and gentle as you do this work. Grant grace to yourself—and to others when they, too, fall short. Life has many chapters. You can write the next few with even more gusto, making sure you are the hero of your own life all the way through.

**To Consider:** Have you ever been to a funeral or celebration of life where the eulogies were full of the person's accomplishments that no one knew about? Everyone says, "Who knew?" You don't want that. Don't wait till life is over to share. You want people to ask you, "What's next?" By sharing now, you can have an even greater impact on so many more lives.

**To Do:** Answer these questions for yourself:

- What recognition do you want to receive?

- What awards do you want to win? Look them up online. What are the criteria? Did you know that most people self-nominate?

- Where do you want to be published? Or which publications do you want to be featured in—the office newsletter, corporate social media, podcasts, mainstream media?

- Who do you want to see you? Find and study the influencers who could truly move things forward for you. How can you get in their orbit? What is their potential agenda? Who knows them already? You're likely closer than you think.

- How can you reframe your "flaws" or mistakes into benefits or attributes?

**To Share:** Share Becky Hemsley's poem "Breathe" with three friends who need it.

# Conclusion
# Call to Greatness

BARBE-NICOLE PONSARDIN wrote this bit of advice to her great-grandchild: "The world is in perpetual motion, and we must invent the things of tomorrow. One must go before others, be determined and exacting, and let your intelligence direct your life. Act with audacity." By this time, Ponsardin had overcome war, a pandemic, and patriarchy to build a champagne empire. She did it by acting with audacity, disregarding the normal restraints, and being bold at a time when she was expected to live by a bourgeois code that forced French women into the shadows of their husbands. She was only twenty-seven when she became a widow—her husband, François Clicquot, died of typhoid fever six years after they married. The Widow Clicquot, as she became known, went on to build one of the largest, most successful, and well-known champagne houses in the world: Veuve Clicquot. She's also credited with major breakthroughs and innovations in the industry. She became the "Grande Dame of Champagne," a legend and a visionary.

Bragging rights are about audacity. It's about owning your worth to get the opportunities you deserve. It's about standing out and fitting in. It's about celebrating both the success and the journey to get there. It's about gratitude, knowing we are thankful to those who have come before. It's about changing systems so we can make a better future. It's about asking *everyone* to show their work instead of letting some people get a free pass while others are told to work harder.

In this era, we must reconsider what we thought we knew and start fresh—not necessarily over but from a pivot point. The path isn't set. The old rules can be reimagined. We can be contributors to more significant partnerships, to pool our resources, but for that to happen, we as individuals need to be seen. For the world of work to gain and keep meaning in people's lives, we must let more people shine with pride. That's what bragging means—for people to shimmer with pride.

For the good girl waiting, reconciling the old rules with the reality of the future may be a challenge. But we must shed what holds us back. I know some of those things are easier to be rid of than others—there's no quick fix when there are cultural and societal norms. Looking at the big picture, though, the behavior of downplaying, deflecting, and self-deprecating doesn't help anyone. Passing over people and insisting they remain hidden gems, or passing over yourself and being reluctant to self-advocate, is a waste to everyone: individuals, companies, society, culture. We're dealing with success that has already happened, and more success will come from it if we share and celebrate it. We can't wait as if life were a dress rehearsal. If we want to be seen and to make a positive change, we must talk about our work and our success to earn social currency, so we can meet the partners who will help us make things happen. Untold opportunities already out there need you.

All of our moments count. Record them. Honor, cherish, and cheer for each one. Don't wait for the perfect milestones to brag.

Talking about success, wisdom, skills, experience, performance, and achievement should be as natural as wanting all of us to thrive. It's a foundational human desire to be seen and heard. And you can be: you have bragging rights.

You are the greatest you in the world. Now you have the tools to tell the world about it.

See you soon. I'll be watching for you.

LISA

# Bonus Material

HERE ARE SOME EXTRA TIPS for how to self-promote and exercise your bragging right.

**Ask for a review:** Reviews are worth gold to everyone, but we tend to think they'll just magically happen. It's like posting on social media: we hope people will comment and engage with our posts, but in turn we don't think our comments, likes, or ratings matter. They do.

The person leaving a review benefits, just as you do. Their name is seen online. They are influencing others with their opinion and can add their own thought leadership. Some people leave reviews as part of their self-promotion tactics.

To ask for your own reviews to use on social media, your website, or as part of your brag files with less angst, automate the process. Craft an initial email template that outlines what you need. Give people all the information they need to make a review quick and easy. After any successful project or initiative, ask for a testimonial by tweaking the email to customize it, then hit send. Don't think too much about it.

And don't forget to thank people for leaving reviews.

**Do your own research:** Another way to establish your authority is to conduct and publish original research. It could be as easy as conducting a three-question survey or as robust as a questionnaire with multiple questions. You can use an online tool to make a multiple-choice form or hire a research company. Depending on your goals, share the information locally, regionally, or internationally. (See the section on visibility fields in chapter 8.) You can publish your findings in your company newsletter, emails, local newspaper, associations, or in a book. You're also putting out your expertise signals at least twice when you do your own research: first, when you ask people to respond to your research, and second, when you publish your findings. It's also a good way to introduce yourself to media producers with topics for an interview.

**Send follow-up emails:** Send follow-up emails after meeting people to cultivate a deeper connection. Everyone knows to do this, but so few people do. The heavy lifting is done after the initial meeting. It's the same thing when you have a conference "best friend." Before you leave the conference, make a date to chat. Most opportunities are lost because of the lack of follow-up.

**Use ownership phrases:** Give yourself authority. People listen closer after you use these set-up phrases:

- **"Something I say often…"** This phrase lets people know that this isn't the first time you've given this consideration; you've been there and done that.

- **"In my experience, 100 percent of the time, this happens…"** The first part of the sentence reminds us that you have experience and the number is solid, not wavering, and it connects our minds to proof and authority. Use this when you want to convince someone of a typical outcome that they should expect by listening to you.

**Don't be a mean girl:** It goes without saying, but just in case: don't be mean when someone else brags. Just ignore it if you don't like it.

**Celebrate the good:** If you abhor talking about yourself, what about celebrating the goodness you give to the world by commenting on the goodness you see in the world?

**Be clear:** If you can, show people. Have some pictures, stories, facts, and figures to tell your story. Don't be vague with terms like "unprecedented growth."

**Reframe:** A brag is not about who you are. It is about your accomplishments. It's not about what is inherent to you, such as intelligence, luck, or good looks. Instead, it's about something you did (hard work, perseverance, innovation, skill). Consider:

- Is this brag my truth?
- Will it help me?
- Will it help others?

Describe an action (how you did the job) and an outcome (proof that you did a good job). If others have helped you, credit them.

**Develop a statement:** Develop a three-part accomplishment statement. Fill in the blanks: *I created _____ that resulted in _____ , enabling _____ to do _____ .*

**Gain some stage time:** One tip I repeatedly gave when all the conferences went online during the COVID-19 pandemic was to take advantage of the "ask a question" portion. In the question box, write your name and your business or division along with one open-ended question, one that does not have a yes or no answer. The moderator or the guest of the conference will say your name as part of the question. It's a low-stakes way to get into the conversation, and it elevates your status. People in my workshops and keynotes followed this advice when it came time for questions, but I'm not sure the rest of the world caught the idea. Use it.

At live conferences, be ready with questions and go up to the microphone. Have a clear, straightforward question and ask it. You can think of this question at home, weeks before the event; you know who is going to be at the event and the gist of what they'll talk about. Have a few back-up questions too. And ask someone to take your photo while you're asking the question so you can post it afterward.

Here are some of my "back-pocket questions":

- What were you thinking about on your way here? (What's your latest thinking?)
- What was your lightning moment?
- Tell us a story that shaped you into who you are today.
- When did you know you had to pivot?
- What do people get wrong?
- What one bit of advice would you give your younger self?
- What should we do first? Or where is a good place to start?
- What's something you wish someone had asked?

Now, take these questions and apply them to yourself. If someone asked them of you, how would you respond?

# Acknowledgments

**HERE'S AN OPPORTUNITY** for me to show off behind-the-scenes bragging rights. I'm here only because of the tremendous efforts of others who helped me. For that, I am thankful.

To my daughter, Elora: You are powerful beyond measure. You are meant to shine, my love. Your presence automatically helps others be brighter. Thank you for having patience with me.

Thank you to Jason Colbert, my husband: You didn't let me shrink or hide when I wanted to while writing this book. You are far stronger than you will ever know. I appreciate you for being brilliant, gorgeous, talented, and fabulous (and for bringing me copious amounts of tea when I was under deadlines).

Thank you to my family near and far, including my mom, Arleen. When I started in TV news, my dad would say to me, "Sparkle, Lisa, sparkle." (It was his spin on what Shirley Temple's mother would say to her before the child megastar of the Depression era performed.)

I can't thank my publishing team at Page Two enough for joining me on this journey. They are by far the experts and visionaries in their field. Thank you to my editor, Kendra Ward, for using your mighty strength of cutting and shaping, all with kindness. To Steph VanderMeulen, for your copyediting skills and catching the grammar slip-ups my broadcast-writing style couldn't see. To project manager Adrineh Der-Boghossian, for keeping the path forward clear. To Meghan O'Neill, for making sure this book is seen far and wide through her marketing guidance. To Stephen George, for being a fantastic cheerleader and having an alert ear for the audiobook. My book shows up as a ten, thanks to designer Taysia Louie. For believing that this book could be great and will help the world, Trena White deserves the spotlight every time someone buys this book.

Thank you to all my interview subjects. There were so many more wise words from you that didn't make it into the book. I promise I will share your knowledge in other ways. I learned so much from you, and I will always be grateful.

Thank you to my cheerleaders, past and present, who encouraged me to write a book: Sara Curleigh-Parsons, Deborah Aarts, Jeffrey Shaw, Leslie Ehm, Erica Ehm, Enette Pauzé, Colleen Moorehead, Marlene Morrison Nicholls, Lisa Applegath, Lauren Perruzza, Laura Reinholz, Mariecris Pagulayan, Cathy Williams, Sharon Gilmour Glover, Erin Dunbar, Stephanie Johansson, Jill McAbe, Vicki Saunders and the community of Coralus, Karen Gill and the community of everywoman, Dr. Rumeet Billan, Ted and Anita Winkle, Alison Winkle, Mary and Jim Colbert, Kelly Bragg, Glenn Bragg, and so many more.

Thank you to everyone who responded to the Bragging Rights research survey. Your thoughts and encouragement made the book even better.

Finally, thank you, dear reader, for joining me on this journey. I know you are powerful beyond measure.

# Notes

### Introduction: A Call to Hidden Gems
*But as Maya Angelou so beautifully puts it:* Dawn Reiss, "Why Maya Angelou Disliked Modesty," *The Atlantic*, June 2, 2014, theatlantic.com/entertainment/archive/2014/06/why-maya-angelou-didnt-believe-in-modesty/371965.

*and included an online survey*: Lisa Bragg, "Survey for Research on Self-Promotion, Bragging, Humility, and Culture," forms.gle/CyscQ5rAgZ8EKBMC8.

### 1: A Case for Bragging
*which was originally a nickname*: "BRAGG. Brag, among the Scandinavians, was the god of eloquence, and the word was anciently used in the sense of eloquent; also, accomplished, brave, daring." In William Arthur, *An Etymological Dictionary of Family and Christian Names: With an Essay on Their Derivation and Import* (New York: Sheldon Blakeman & Co., 1857), 77, archive.org/details/etymologicaldict00arth/page/76/mode/2up?ref=ol&q=bragg.

*Success can come at any time*: Albert-László Barabási, "The Real Relationship between Your Age and Success," posted July 2009, TEDxMidAtlantic, TED video, 16:07, ted.com/talks/albert_laszlo_barabasi_the_real_relationship_between_your_age_and_your_chance_of_success.

*In 1325, "brag" meant "proud"*: M.A.C. de Vaan, "The Etymology of English 'To Brag' and Old Icelandic 'Bragr,'" *Nowele: North-Western European Language Evolution* 41 (2002): 45–58, hdl.handle.net/1887/14140.

*"the justified love of oneself"*: Richard Taylor, *Restoring Pride: The Lost Virtue of Our Age* (Buffalo, NY: Prometheus Books, 1995), n.p.

*When we think of the negativity*: Collins Dictionary, s.v. "self-aggrandizement (n.)," collinsdictionary.com/dictionary/english/self-aggrandizement.

*"You see, I have no patience with modesty"*: Reiss, "Why Maya Angelou Disliked Modesty."

*One dictionary defines it as*: Cambridge Dictionary, s.v. "bragging rights (n.)," dictionary.cambridge.org/dictionary/english/bragging-rights.

*Your bragging rights are*: The Britannica Dictionary, s.v. "bragging rights (n.)," britannica.com/dictionary/bragging-rights.

## 2: A Legacy of Hiding

*As novelist William Gibson said*: Nicholas Davis, "What Is the Fourth Industrial Revolution?" World Economic Forum, January 19, 2016, weforum.org/agenda/2016/01/what-is-the-fourth-industrial-revolution.

*We're now into the "fourth revolution"*: Davis, "What Is the Fourth Industrial Revolution?"

*Clark talked about the relative ease*: Dorie Clark, interview by the author, June 30, 2022.

*The team found that women*: See "The Scully Effect: I Want to Believe in STEM," research by 21st Century Fox, Geena Davis Institute on Gender in Media, and J. Walter Thompson Intelligence, seejane.org/research-informs-empowers/the-scully-effect-i-want-to-believe-in-stem.

*"It's been twelve years since I became"*: America Ferrera, "My Identity Is a Superpower—Not an Obstacle," posted May 2019, TED2019, TED video, 13:53, ted.com/talks/america_ferrera_my_identity_is_a_superpower_not_an_obstacle.

*"I'd tell you in a conversation"*: Lisa Mattam and Lisa Bragg (host), "Sustainable Beauty: More Than Just Skin Deep," season 3, episode 6, July 28, 2022, in Bold(h)er, produced by BMO for Women, podcast, 43 mins., bmoforwomen.libsyn.com/sustainable-beauty-more-than-just-skin-deep.

*Leaders set norms*: Annie Neimand, "Changing Culture by Changing Norms," UNHCR Innovation Service, Medium.com, September 2, 2020, medium.com/bending-the-arc/changing-culture-by-changing-norms-64b79c77a14b.

*However, a US survey*: SHRM, "Survey: 84 Percent of U.S. Workers Blame Bad Managers for Creating Unnecessary Stress," August 12, 2020, shrm.org/about-shrm/press-room/press-releases/pages/survey-84-percent-of-us-workers-blame-bad-managers-for-creating-unnecessary-stress-.aspx.

"*Bragging about yourself violates norms*": Adam Grant, "My Festivus Grievances about Online Comments," *Psychology Today*, December 24, 2013, psychologytoday.com/ca/blog/give-and-take/201312/my-festivus-grievances-about-online-comments.

*according to the research*: Adam Grant, "Originals: How Non-Conformists Move the World," presentation and Q&A, WPO Conference (online), July 22–23, 2020.

*when some audiences see a woman*: Lola Akinmade Åkerström, interview by the author, May 10, 2022.

*It just happens much earlier*: Bonnie Marcus, *Not Done Yet!: How Women Over 50 Regain Their Confidence and Claim Workplace Power* (Vancouver: Page Two Books, 2021); Peter Clayton, "Not Done Yet! How Women Over 50 Regain Their Confidence and Claim Workplace Power," interview with Bonnie Marcus, March 10, 2021, YouTube video, 33:09, youtu.be/QjSl-qyb5xY?t=1597.

## 3: How Power Plays In

*Consider this from Carol Dweck*: Katy Kay and Claire Shipman, *The Confidence Code: The Science and Art of Self-Assurance—What Women Should Know* (New York: HarperCollins, 2018), 90.

"*I thought it was unfair because*": Mary Ann Sieghart, interview by the author, July 4, 2022.

"*I've come to recognize that*": NPR, "Adam Galinksy: What Drives Us to Speak Up?" TED Radio Hour, April 7, 2017, transcript of interview with Guy Raz, 12 mins., npr.org/transcripts/522857511.

*Stefan Scheidt defines facilitators*: Stefan Scheidt, *Personal Branding of Top Managers*, December 10, 2021, PhD thesis, ris.utwente.nl/ws/portalfiles/portal/268025014/Thesis_Stefan_Scheidt.pdf.

"*While team success requires diversity and balance*": Roger Dooley, "The Science of Success with Alberto-Laszlo Barabasi," December 17, 2020, rogerdooley.com/barabasi-success-formula.

"*Particularly shocking to me*": Kathy Caprino, "An International HR Leader Publicly and Bravely Admits Her Bias Against Women Leaders," *Forbes*, September 24, 2016, forbes.com/sites/kathycaprino/2016/09/24/an-international-hr-leader-publicly-and-bravely-admits-her-bias-against-women-leaders.

"*Mentally flip whomever you're dealing with*": Karen Pressner, "Flip It to Test It," November 4, 2016, TEDxBasel, TED video, 8:49, tedxbasel.com/txb-blog/2016/11/4/tedxbasel-talks-15-kristen-pressner.

## 4: How We Are at Odds

"*Sawubona, we see you*": "Sawubona, We See You," September 23, 2019, TEDxMahikeng, TED video, 13:18, youtube.com/watch?v=xpqU9 MtL8MI&t=4s.

*the culture of bragging was slowly changing*: Panel of Japanese women, including Ayumi Nishimura, Erika Hirose, Akane Takahashi, and Harumi Gondo, interview by the author, March 3, 2022.

*the "What will people say?" rule of action*: Piyali Mandal, interview by the author, April 21, 2022.

"*It stopped me from*": Beth Kowitt, "Former PepsiCo CEO Indra Nooyi Explains Why She 'Never, Ever, Ever' Asked for a Raise," *Fortune*, October 8, 2021, fortune.com/2021/10/08/indra-nooyi-ever-asked-for-a-raise.

"*[There was the] combination of academic stereotypes*: Jenny Chen, interview by the author, September 8, 2022.

"*When you sit with an Elder or Wisdom Keeper*": Brenda MacIntyre (Medicine Song Woman), interview by the author, April 9, 2022.

"*I recently heard someone say*": Rumeet Billan, "The Tallest Poppy Data Made Me Angry," Canadian HR Reporter, September 24, 2018, hrreporter.com/news/hr-news/the-tallest-poppy-data-made-me-angry-opinion/283479.

*People usually get a pass*: Emelia Sam, interview by the author, April 14, 2022.

## 5: Programming Is Reality and Myth

*She kept her mother's voice*: Vivian Pickard with Lisa Bragg (host), "You Belong in the Room," season 2, episode 14, December 16, 2021, in *Bold(h)er*, produced by BMO for Women, podcast, 38 mins., bmoforwomen.libsyn.com/you-belong-in-the-room.

*The path looks like an S-curve*: To learn more about S-curve thinking, see Whitney Johnson, "Manage Your Organization as a Portfolio of Learning Curves," *Harvard Business Review*, January–February 2022, hbr.org/2022/01/manage-your-organization-as-a-portfolio-of-learning-curves.

*Women's leadership expert*: Tara Sophia Mohr, "Why Women Don't Apply for Jobs unless They're 100 Percent Qualified," *Harvard Business Review*, August 25, 2014, hbr.org/2014/08/why-women-dont-apply-for-jobs-unless-theyre-100-qualified.

"*It's an English idea*": Mark Bowden, interview by the author, August 30, 2022.

*A Research Brief article*: Brad Bushman and Sophie Kjaevik, "Narcissistic People Aren't Just Full of Themselves—New Research Finds They're More Likely to Be Aggressive and Violent," The Conversation, Research Brief, May 25, 2021, theconversation.com/narcissistic-people-arent-just-full-of-themselves-new-research-finds-theyre-more-likely-to-be-aggressive-and-violent-155815.

"*Narcissism may be a functional*": Keith W. Campbell, "Is Narcissism Really So Bad?" *Psychological Inquiry* 12, no. 4 (October 2001): 214–16, researchgate.net/publication/274006428_Is_Narcissism_Really_So_Bad.

"*Shyness is about the fear*": Susan Cain with Chris Anderson (host), "What's the Difference Between Shyness and Introversion? And How Can Companies Help Introverts Thrive? A Q&A with Susan Cain," transcript excerpt from *The TED Interview*, podcast, Ideas.TED.com, July 29, 2019, ideas.ted.com/whats-the-difference-between-shyness-and-introversion-and-how-can-companies-help-introverts-thrive-a-qa-with-susan-cain.

## 6: The Need to Partner

*In reality, underground*: Suzanne Simard, "Mother Tree," posted by Dan McKinney, December 13, 2011, YouTube video, 4:40, youtube.com/watch?v=-8SORM4dyG8&t=85s.

"*Identity can and should also be used*": Hatch Network, "Deep Dive with Jacqueline Novogratz," Manifesto for a Moral Revolution: Global Living Room, July 8, 2020, Vimeo video, 22:13, hatchexperience.org/global-living-room-15-manifesto-for-a-moral-revolution.

*His definition of success*: Albert-László Barabási, "Introduction," *The Formula: The Universal Laws of Success* (New York: Little, Brown and Company, 2018), online, formula.barabasi.com/intro.html.

*Performance is what you do*: Barabási, "The Real Relationship."

*Jacki Zehner, an investor and former partner*: Jacki Zehner, "Sistering Up: But First, Canapé Anyone?" LinkedIn, SheMoney newsletter, April 30, 2021, linkedin.com/pulse/sistering-up-first-canapé-anyone-jacki-zehner.

*Coined by writer Ann Friedman*: For more on shine theory, see shinetheory.com/what-is-shine-theory.

*psychologist Catherine Chambliss found*: "The Role of Freudenfreude and Schadenfreude in Depression," *World Journal of Psychiatry and Mental Health Research* 2, no. 1 (2018): 1009, remedypublications.com/open-access/the-role-of-freudenfreude-and-schadenfreude-indepression-277.pdf.

"When someone demonstrates joy": Brené Brown, *Atlas of the Heart: Mapping Meaningful Connection and the Language of Human Experience* (New York: Random House, 2021), 37.

she told me that as an adult: Vicky Saunders, interview by the author, February 25, 2022.

"Haters aren't something to be feared": Ann Friedman, "Haters Gonna Hate. What's a Woman to Do about It?" *The Cut*, January 31, 2013, thecut.com/2013/01/haters-gonna-hate-whats-a-woman-to-do.html.

"I understand that I'm supposed to": "Gloria Steinhem Visits St. Mary's College," St. Mary's College of California, News, n.d., stmarys-ca.edu/gloria-steinem-visits-saint-marys-college.

Set up a "Bragging Rights" session: This is an adaptation of "The Holy Trinity" exercise by C.K. Lim and K. Suh, taken from *Widening the Lens: 2019 Net Impact Conference*, keynote presented at TCF Center, Detroit, Michigan, October 2019.

## 7: How to Self-Promote

"You have to show up as a ten": Pickard with Bragg, "You Belong in the Room."

"What a weekend!": Cranla Warren, LinkedIn post, September 2002, linkedin.com/feed/update/urn:li:activity:6977572836492152832.

"By increasing the number": Niro Sivanathan, "What If Your Arguments Don't Add Up?" TEDxLondonBusinessSchool, posted June 13, 2019, YouTube video, 10:52, youtu.be/hkFCu6K8Ghw.

"you can ascertain what's important": Liz Wiseman, "Why You Should Think of Passion as a Verb—Not a Noun," *Harvard Business Review*, August 19, 2022, hbr.org/2022/08/why-you-should-think-of-passion-as-a-verb-not-a-noun.

the "model herself spoke": Malcolm Gladwell, "True Colors: Hair Dye and the Hidden History of Postwar America," *New Yorker*, March 14, 1999, newyorker.com/magazine/1999/03/22/true-colors.

It now alternates between: See "Because You're Worth It," lorealparisusa.com/because-youre-worth-it.

"I know it might feel odd": Whitney Johnson, interview by the author, May 19, 2022.

"I was a student at Harvard Business School": Lisa Bragg and Andrea Wojnicki (host), "Bragging, Self-Promotion, and Your Personal Brand," episode 105, July 11, 2022, in *Talk About Talk*, podcast, 39:21, talkabouttalk.com/105-bragging.

*She discovered that*: Amanda Nimon-Peters, "9 Principals of Persuasion for the 21st Century," AACSB, July 19, 2022, aacsb.edu/insights/articles/2022/07/9-principles-of-persuasion-for-the-21st-century.

*In late summer 2022*: Lisa LaFlamme (@LisaLaFlamme_), "I have some news...." Twitter, August 15, 2022, twitter.com/LisaLaFlamme_/status/1559238644317167618.

*Just fifty-one minutes after*: Omar Sachedina (@omarsachedina), "I am honoured to be following in the footsteps of Lisa LaFlamme and Lloyd Robertson. So excited to be working with our incredibly talented team in this new role!" Twitter, August 15, 2022, twitter.com/omarsachedina/status/1559251523493928962.

*"There's a thing called FIGJAM"*: Dee Dee Taylor Eustace, interview by the author, August 15, 2022.

*In her Netflix special*: *Nanette*, directed by Madeleine Perry and Jon Olb, screenplay by Hannah Gadsby, featuring Hannah Gadsby, June 19, 2018, on Netflix, 18:00.

*Moral grandstanding involves outdoing*: Brandon Warmke, "The Psychology of Moral Grandstanding," Big Think, n.d., video, 7:10, bigthink.com/neuropsych/the-psychology-of-moral-grandstanding.

*"when you brag your own disaster"*: Jenn Doll, "Hello Underbrag, the Best Dang Bragging in the Whole Wide World," *The Atlantic*, August 14, 2012, theatlantic.com/culture/archive/2012/08/hello-underbrag-best-dang-bragging-whole-wide-world/324722; see also HBO, "*Sex and the City*: Berger Dumps Carrie with a Post-it Note (Season 6 Clip)," YouTube video, 3:23, youtube.com/watch?v=2q-XzdrqpsM.

*One of the cofounders, Leticia Gasca*: Lavinia Tuturas, "Failure Culture," LinkedIn post, September 5, 2019, linkedin.com/pulse/failure-culture-lavinia-tuturas.

*The* New York Times Magazine: "Profiles in Self-Promotion," *New York Times Magazine*, March 2, 1997, nytimes.com/1997/03/02/magazine/profiles-in-self-promotion.html.

*A study on the workplace*: University of British Columbia, "Being Paranoid about Office Politics Can Make You a Target," *Science Daily*, July 31, 2012, sciencedaily.com/releases/2012/07/120731135008.htm.

## 8: Brag with Purpose

*"I would share with my parents"*: Jacqueline Kerr, interview by the author, April 26, 2022.

### 9: Know What Makes You Remarkable

*"I was brought up in a world"*: Joe Foster, *Shoemaker: The Untold Story of the British Family Firm That Became a Global Brand* (London, UK: Simon and Schuster, 2021), 5.

*Social psychologists call this*: Geoffrey Leonardelli, Cynthia Pickett, and Marilynn Brewer, "Optimal Distinctiveness Theory: A Framework for Social Identity, Social Cognition, and Intergroup Relations," *Advances in Experimental Social Psychology* 43 (2010): 63–113, doi.org/10.1016/S0065-2601(10)43002-6.

*whom they define as "those indispensable colleagues"*: Liz Wiseman and Lauren Hancock, "Impact Players of the Workplace," *Leader to Leader* no. 103 (Winter 2021): 31–37, doi.org/10.1002/ltl.20621.

*liked to tell the story*: Rick Wartzman, "Some Words of Wisdom from Peter Drucker to My Daughter," *Time*, May 7, 2014, time.com/89695/some-words-of-wisdom-from-peter-drucker-to-my-daughter.

### 10: Own Your Knowledgeable Authority

*"the difference between saying"*: Seth Godin, "A Point of View," *Seth's Blog*, seths.blog/2017/12/a-point-of-view.

*"We create interest"*: Karen Eber, "81 Minutes," Eber Leadership Group, *Brain Food* (blog), kareneber.com/blog/81-minutes.

*In her TED Talk, Eber says*: Karen Eber, "How Your Brain Responds to Stories—And Why They're Crucial for Leaders," TEDxPurdueU, posted January 2021, TED video, 13.54, ted.com/talks/karen_eber_how_your_brain_responds_to_stories_and_why_they_re_crucial_for_leaders.

*"Lesson learned"*: Mordy Golding, LinkedIn post, September 2022, linkedin.com/posts/mordygolding_strategy-presentations-behumble-activity-6972192993030111233-KBbq.

*Research shows that*: Kate McLean et al., "Redemptive Stories and Those Who Tell Them Are Preferred in the U.S.," *Psychology* 6, no. 1 (2020): 39, online.ucpress.edu/collabra/article/6/1/39/114472/Redemptive-Stories-and-Those-Who-Tell-Them-are.

*"The redemption story is American optimism"*: Julie Beck, "Life's Stories," *The Atlantic*, August 10, 2015, theatlantic.comhealtharchive/2015/08/life-stories-narrative-psychology-redemption-mental-health/400796.

*Here's an example of a story*: Lisa Bragg, LinkedIn post, September 2022, linkedin.com/feed/update/urn:li:activity:6971532710682976256.

## 11: Know Who You Are

*her cheerleaders have sometimes come*: Sharon Heck, interview by the author, December 4, 2021.

## 12: Help People Talk about You

*an excellent exposé on fake followers and their effect*: Nicholas Confessore, Gabriel J.X. Dance, Richard Harris, and Mark Hansen, "The Follower Factory," *New York Times*, January 27, 2018, nytimes.com/interactive/2018/01/27/technology/social-media-bots.html.

*The Joe Foster of our time noted*: Foster, *Shoemaker*, 14.

## 13: Lead Others to Shine

*"the tendency for positive impressions"*: Wikipedia, s.v. "halo effect," en.wikipedia.org/wiki/Halo_effect.

*she used to hide at the back*: Mita Mallick, interview by the author, April 26, 2022.

*"We have a responsibility to lean"*: Emily Feairs, interview by the author, May 11, 2022.

*Researchers at Cornell University*: Jesse Walker, Stephanie J. Tepper, and Thomas Gilovich, "People Are More Tolerant of Inequality When It Is Expressed in Terms of Individuals Rather Than Groups at the Top," *PNAS* 118, no. 43 (2021), doi.org/10.1073/pnas.2100430118.

*It's an intervention designed by researchers*: Catherine Chambliss, Amy Hartl, Jenna Bowker, and Emily Short, "Reducing Depression via Brief Interpersonal Mutuality Training (IMT): A Randomized Control Trial," *International Journal of Health Sciences* 2, no. 1 (March 2014): 19–28, ijhsnet.com/journals/ijhs/Vol_2_No_1_March_2014/2.pdf.

*Another term from the same research*: Chambliss et al., "Reducing Depression."

## 14: No Longer a Hidden Gem

*"You have to try your hardest"*: Tina Fey, *Bossypants* (New York: Reagan Arthur Books, 2011).

*As reported in a 2022 article*: Matthew J. Easterbrook, "People Like Us...," The British Psychological Society, *The Psychologist*, May 26, 2022, bps.org.uk/psychologist/people-us.

*A course on influence*: A. Martinez with Zoe Chance, "Yale Professor Teaches Influence and She Says It's Your Superpower," NPR, *Morning Edition*, interview transcript, February 2, 2022, npr.org/2022/02/02/1077522578/yale-professor-teaches-influence-and-she-says-its-your-superpower.

"*There can be a hundred people*": The Fab Teacher, "Lady Gaga Saying 'There Can Be a Hundred People in the Room' For One Minute Straight," October 8, 2018, YouTube video, 1:30, youtube.com/watch?v=iRxsX_3Otjs&t=3s.

"*There is an element of imposter syndrome*": Becky Hemsley, interview by the author, March 1, 2022.

"*Breathe*": Becky Hemsley, "Breathe," etsy.com/uk/shop/TalkingtotheWild.

## Conclusion: Call to Greatness

"*The world is in perpetual motion*": Tilar J. Mazzeo, *The Widow Clicquot: The Story of a Champagne Empire and the Woman Who Ruled It* (New York: Harper Business, 2009), 235.

# About the Author

**LISA BRAGG** has devoted her life to helping people be seen and heard sharing their value with the world.

Through Bragging Rights and her other programs, she collaborates with leaders, experts, and visionaries to help people stand out and fit in by talking about success. She shares her methods and frameworks through keynotes, workshops, and programs.

Bragg also works as a consultant, thinking partner, and advisor to companies of all sizes. She turns business problems into assets and complex ideas into engaging stories.

She is also the founder and former CEO of the award-winning MediaFace, one of the world's first content creation companies, which she launched in her basement. MediaFace is a two-time recipient of the Growth 500 Award for the fastest-growing business in Canada. She is a former TV news anchor, reporter, videographer, and show host who has covered a wide range of stories from international events to the lemonade stand just around the corner.

# OF COURSE! THERE'S MORE!

To find out what courses, workshops, and keynotes I currently offer, visit **LisaBragg.com**.

## To Bulk Order Books

Contact me to find out about discounts and special offers that can help you buy copies of *Bragging Rights* for your entire team or organization. We can even partner to create a customized edition that includes a foreword from your CEO or other leader.

Please write a review of *Bragging Rights* on your preferred platform. Remember, this is an opportunity for you to brag and self-promote, too, as people will see your generous comment. Thank you!

And keep in touch. You can reach me at:

- hello@lisabragg.com
- linkedin.com/in/lisabragg
- @thatlisabragg
- @ThatLisaBragg

Tag your posts with **#BraggingRights** and I will see them.

Printed in Great Britain
by Amazon